Diamondfield

Finding the real Jack Davis

Jack Davis in 1905. The Goldfield Chronicle.

Diamondfield

♦

Finding the real Jack Davis

Laura
Hope you enjoy the Read

Max C. Black

Max C Black

RIDENBAUGH PRESS
Carlton, Oregon

DIAMONDFIELD: FINDING THE REAL JACK DAVIS

For more information, contact Ridenbaugh Press, P.O. Box 834, Carlton OR 97111.

Printed and bound in the United States of America.

First edition May 2013

10 9 8 7 6 5 4 3 2 1

Library of Congress Cataloging in Publication Data

Max C. Black

Diamondfield: Finding the Real Jack Davis

Bibliography

1. Idaho Politics and Government. 2. Idaho-Economy. 3. Idaho-History.

I. Black, Max C. II. Title.

ISBN-10 978-0-945648-06-2 (softbound)

Cover illustrations:

Ridenbaugh Press
P.O. Box 834, Carlton OR 97111
Phone (503) 852-0010
www.ridenbaugh.com
stapilus@ridenbaugh.com

Contents

Preface

Jackson Lee Davis, alias "Diamondfield Jack," entered Idaho on the slopes of Shoshone Basin in the middle of a cattlemen-sheepmen range war, as an enforcer for the Sparks-Harrell Cattle Company. He was a brash young man with a gun, handed the job of enforcer on one side of a range war. What could go wrong?

Reprisal, to begin with—reprisal brought upon himself because of his mouth, the prejudice of a community, competing lawyers, and political parties, as well as competing newspapers.

It was the time in America's history between the social/economic dislocations caused by the Civil War, and the boom years of the industrial revolution. A most compelling influence on many of those individuals and groups, being part of the settling of the West, was the lingering attitude where justice was often settled by the wearing of the gun.

The Diamondfield Jack story has become irresistible, not only as a classic tale of the Old West, and not only as a compelling tale of battling interests with striking personalities at its core, but also because of its air of mystery. Repeatedly convicted of a double murder in high-profile legal actions, Jack eventually was pardoned and released. But what was the truth? Was Jack guilty or not?

Over the years Diamondfield Jack has become the subject of an endless stream of articles, essays, even full-length biographies. Fact and myth have blended together, distorting and obscuring the reality of Jack's world and his actions. Much of what has been written about Jack has come from second-hand accounts which were themselves based on often questionable sources. There's some irony in this, since the "Diamondfield" nickname reflected Davis' own periodic propensity for exaggeration and distortion: His own story has fallen victim to the same thing.

This book is an attempt to strip away the myth and recreate the Jack Davis story as it actually was. New technology has given us the ability to discover and retrieve previously buried information. Access to digitalized newspapers and public recorders has opened up more than four decades of history, and far more details of the life of this extraordinary man. The excellent and amazing staff at the Idaho Historical Society enabled me to search and find an inordinate amount of information about the Jack Davis affair in Idaho. Locating and having access to the court records and James Hawley's legal papers led to some fascinating discoveries.

Much of Jack's life still lay ahead the day he walked out of prison in Idaho, and a great part of those decades to come was as remarkable as what came before.

The stories of Jack's life in and around Idaho's criminal justice system include little about his later years in Nevada. I turned my research to the Nevada Historical Society hoping they would have some records pertaining to "Diamondfield" Jack Davis. Both the Reno and Carson City offices were eager to assist in my search. The Reno staff found some information but referred me to the Carson City office where a more complete file on the subject may be found. After a brief search, by the Carson City staff, enough information was found for me to justify a trip to Carson City. However it was suggested, by their staff I contact the Central Nevada Historical Society at Tonopah where an even more complete file could be located.

I contacted the Tonopah office and Eva La Rue, one of the curators, answered the phone and was personally familiar with at least a couple of stories involving "Diamondfield" Jack Davis. She had co-authored an article about Jack in the 2003 summer edition of Central Nevada's *GLORIOUS PAST,* a publication of the Central Nevada Historical Society. When I went to Tonopah a short time later Eva was able to locate seventy-five separate pieces of information beginning with Jack's arrival in Tonopah in 1903. The information was largely newspaper articles from twenty different papers in Nevada during the first number of years he resided in Nevada. Within the next three months I was able to collect over two hundred and fifty newspaper stories and references about Jack's forty years in and out Nevada. Good fortune found Jack in Nevada making millions, elected mayor of a city, Nevada's delegate to the National Cattlemen's Association Conference, business partner with two governors and three future U.S. senators from Nevada, preventing a lynching by a mob, and getting shot in the face by a would be assassin. During these years Jack reached celebrity status and resulted in being the subject of hundreds of newspaper articles across the United States.

PART ONE

Trials in Idaho

High desert (1895)

The landscape has not changed much.

It looks as it did in the 1860s and 1870s: High mountains presiding over treeless valleys, covered with an abundance of sagebrush and grass. Early immigrants viewed this landscape carefully as they passed through the valleys of southern Idaho and northeast Nevada.

Water is scarce on the desert, with limited rainfall during summer months; most of the moisture arrives during the harsh winters. Water seeping from mountain springs forms small streams which meander across the valley floor until they join a larger stream or, in many cases, just sink back into the ground. These springs and small streams help generate rich meadow lands from which the ranchers can cut grass and hay for winter feed.

When the pioneer immigrants wound their way across the vast expanse of sage brush and grassland on the California Trail in the 1840s and 1850s, they had no idea of the richness of the soils and forage resources under their feet. Their sole aim then was to quicken their footsteps across the nothingness and reach California. A few travelers broke down or in some cases became too sick to travel on, only to stay behind and discover the gold and fortunes they were seeking in California.

The grass lands of northeast Nevada and southern Idaho offered a different opportunity for the strong-spirited agricultural-minded pioneers. It was only a matter of time before a few of those men and women who had made the trek to California returned to the area, bringing with them with the wealth or disappointment they accumulated in the Golden State. They discovered that the seeming nothingness on which they had camped along their trek west was, in fact, an exceptional grazing resource to fatten their cattle for market, but like the gold and silver found in veins in the mountains, these grazing resources rapidly depleted. Unlike the gold and silver however, the rich grasslands could be restored if managed properly.

The first stage of development and exploitation of the sagebrush grassland regions of northern Nevada and southern Idaho occurred between the Civil War and the end of the nineteenth century. During those decades, the resource was overgrazed, and its ability to reproduce depleted. In his book *Cattle in the Cold Desert*, James A. Young describes this region from both a scientific and historical perspective, weaving together the science and the history of how man and his herds and flocks of domestic animals exploited the forage resources of a pristine environment. From the 1860s through the twentieth century, men took advantage of this environment to develop one of the largest cattle operations in America. They accumulated fortunes, but sometimes lost those fortunes just as quickly because of forces of nature over which they had little control. They soon learned that, in order to preserve this precious resource, they needed to give back to the land as well as take from it.

Jasper Harrell bought his first ranch in the early 1870s in the Thousand Springs Valley, north of Wells, Nevada. "As Jasper was developing his operation two other men, John Sparks and John Tinnin, came into the country and bought out Jasper's interests. Sparks and Tinnin recognized the potential wealth of the region's resources and continued to expand Jasper Harrell's operation, creating one of the largest cattle empires in America. Various reports at the time estimated the cattle herd to be as large as 175,000 head, plus thousands of horses. At the height of the operation Sparks' and Tannin's holdings encompassed an area more than 100 miles square, with more than 25 operating ranches that extended from just below Rock Creek, Idaho, southeast to the Nevada/Utah border, then meandering 90 miles west towards Wells, Nevada. The western boundary extended as far west as the Jarbidge Mountains and into Owyhee County, Idaho. Driving through the vast region of northern Nevada and southern Idaho today, with its miles of desolate desert landscape, it is hard to imagine or believe the history and wealth emanating from this cattle empire.

During the same time that northern Nevada and western Idaho's Cassia County were developing into cattle country, eastern Cassia County and the community of Oakley were developing a sheep industry.

Large herds of sheep were being driven from northwestern Utah into the region to take advantage of the grazing benefits. The same story was repeated many times across the West, as sheep herds and cattle herds attempted to occupy the same range land.

Because the cattlemen were generally the first on the range, they felt they had a priority grazing right to the public range lands. But the sheepmen held that they had an equal right to graze their sheep there—it was after all, public land. Conflict was inevitable, as both cattlemen and sheepmen fought bitterly to maintain what they both perceived to be their priority grazing rights.

Abraham Lincoln expressed it well as he was walking along a sidewalk towards his home keeping his two howling boys, Willie and Tad, separated. When a neighbor asked, "Why, Mr. Lincoln, what's the matter?" he replied, "Just what's the matter with the whole world. I've got three walnuts and each wants two."

The conflict intensified between the two sides as a result of short water years between 1886 and 1889, followed by severe snows during the devastating winter of 1889-1890. The low water years resulted in sharply reduced plant growth; this was followed by a year of deep snow and below-freezing temperatures that prevented the animals from finding what little grass may have been available

During that longer-than-normal winter, with temperatures dropping as low as -45 degrees, cattle losses were reported to be 50 to 70 percent in many herds, and as high as 95 percent in some. The sheep herds survived those bitter conditions much better than the cattle. The range sheep were wintered exclusively on desert ranges where they were better adapted to the environment and forage base. Sheep are able to obtain their water needs from the snow and their feed needs from scantier foliage sources. Thus, the net immediate effect of the white winter was freedom for the range sheep industry to expand without competition from previously established cattle herds. Tensions increased as the cattlemen struggled to recover from their losses, reestablish their herds, and at the same time protect previously controlled range lands. Both sides became more resolute to stand their ground.

By the early part of 1895 tensions between the cattlemen and the sheep men increased despite what the cattlemen thought was an understanding that the sheep men would not graze their sheep west of an arbitrary line referred to as the Deadline Ridge. The Deadline Ridge ran north and south 15 or 20 miles west of Oakley, Idaho. It was used as the boundary, intended to keep the sheep men east of the ridge and keep the cattlemen on the range west of the line. The cattlemen seemed to understand this boundary but the sheep men were not so accepting, and continued to graze their sheep on public lands to the west of the ridge—not only was it public land, it was also some of the best grazing range land in the area.

In an effort to protect what the cattlemen felt was their priority grazing right, the Sparks-Harrell Cattle Company hired Jack Davis to work up in the Shoshone Valley under the guise of herding some of their cattle. In reality, Jack was tasked with keeping sheep men from bringing their herds onto what the cattlemen felt to be their range land. Words had failed to keep the sheep men from moving westward, and as so often happened during these cattle/sheep conflicts, words turned to gun fire.

Following the death of two young men, Davis was charged with murder and a legal battle between some of Idaho's most eminent lawyers ensued. William E. Borah, later Idaho's U.S. Senator, was one of the special prosecutors hired to assist John C. Rogers, Cassia County's Prosecuting Attorney. James H. Hawley, later governor of the state of Idaho, was the lead defense attorney, along with his law partner, Kirkland I. Perky. The well-known lawyers, plus another special prosecutor by the name of Orlando W. Powers, who had served on the supreme court in Utah Territory, gave the case a high profile. Public interest around the state was high, but in and around Cassia County the interest was personal, pitting neighbor against neighbor, community against community. Over the next six years the case moved from Idaho's lower courts to the Idaho Supreme Court, to the Federal District Court and then to the U. S. Supreme Court. The last resort for Hawley was the Idaho Board of Pardons.

The primary sources of information for this book about the Diamondfield Jack legal proceedings were James H. Hawley's own legal papers, located in the Archives of the Idaho State Historical Society. Newspaper accounts from the period, found in the files of the *Idaho Statesman*, the *Albion General News*, the *Oakley Herald*, and other early newspapers of the period, were also most helpful in providing details of the personal and emotional aspects of the case.

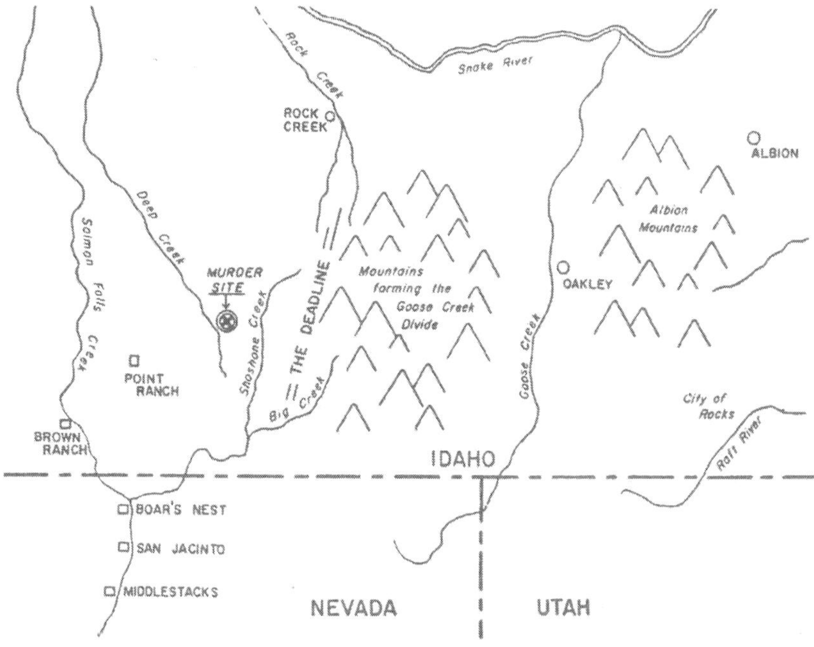

The tri-state area which formed the setting for the Diamondfield Jack case.

The area shown in the above map is southeast of Rogerson, Idaho, north of Wells, Nevada and west of Albion, Idaho.

A grisly discovery (1896)

On the morning of February 16, 1896, Ted Severe, a young sheep herder from Oakley, rode his horse to the top of a low hill and stopped to survey the countryside near the location where he and his herding partner had just established their new campsite.

Severe estimated that his new camp was located two to three miles from the camp of a friend. Severe decided to ride over the hill to visit the neighboring sheep camp where both the friend and a recent acquaintance from Oakley were tending a band of sheep. As Severe surveyed the landscape of the surrounding area from a low ridge, he noticed that the herd of sheep from that neighboring sheep camp were scattered and appeared to be wandering. Severe looked for the herders but could not see a sign of even one, and it appeared that there was no one attending the sheep. He could see their camp wagon but no one was in sight.

Sensing that something was wrong, Severe rode down to the camp to investigate. He yelled out and asked if anyone was home, but no one responded. The sight of two dogs tied to the rear wheel of the wagon, apparently starving and hardly able to bark, increased his apprehension. Good dogs are an important part in the sheepherder's life; to neglect one's dogs would be almost unthinkable. The situation looked grim, and as Severe dismounted and approached the camp wagon his sense of trouble only grew stronger. When he stepped up onto the tongue of the wagon to peek inside, his worst fears were confirmed: a body lay motionless on the bed at the rear of the wagon.

As soon as Severe entered the wagon he recognized the body as that of Daniel Cummins, a young man who had recently replaced his uncle at the camp. His body was lying across the end of the bed fully clothed, and the front of his shirt was bloody. Lifting the shirt, Severe could see what appeared to be a bullet wound in the young man's stomach. While he was examining Cummins's body he realized that another body was also lying on the bed, covered over with a blanket. When he lifted the cover, Severe recognized it to be that of John Wilson, his friend from

Oakley. His shirt likewise was soaked with blood, from what appeared to be a gunshot to the chin, a wound that resulted in considerable bleeding to the face and shoulder areas of his body. The shock of finding the two bodies left him numb and wondering what to do next. He knew he had to return to his own camp and tell his partner about the grisly discovery. In his excitement to get back to his camp, Severe mounted his horse and rode away, forgetting to care for the two dogs that were tied to the wheels of the camp wagon. He later remembered noticing that one of them had been gnawing on a harness lying under the wagon and consoled himself with the thought that they would have been able to eat snow for water.[1]

After returning to his camp, the decision was made by Severe for Noel Carlson, Severe's 19-year-old herding partner, to ride the 50-some miles over to Oakley to notify the families of the two young men as well as to inform Sheriff Harvey L. Perkins in Albion, the county seat.

A canvas cover camp wagon similar to the one used by Wilson & Cummins. (courtesy, David and Jeannie Eigures)

1 Ted Severe's testimony during Davis' trial.

As soon as Carlson left for Oakley, Severe rode over to a nearby camp to notify Davis Hunter, a neighboring shepherd. Hunter's camp was four or five miles west of Severe's camp. Upon hearing the news, Hunter rode back over to the camp of the two victims to investigate. He had been over to the boys' camp to visit them not too long before, so he was very anxious to go to the scene and investigate for himself. Hunter brought the two dogs back to his camp and after giving them water and food it appeared that they would be fine.

Davis Hunter, as it turned out, was the last person to see the two victims alive, other than the perpetrator of the killing.

Twelve days earlier, on February 4th, Hunter had to make a trip to Oakley to get supplies and attend to some personal business. Early on the morning of the 4th, Hunter went to Wilson's camp to pick up his two-wheeled cart, which Wilson had borrowed a few weeks earlier to make a similar trip for supplies. Hunter testified at the Davis trial that upon arriving at the Wilson camp all seemed to be well with Wilson and Cummins. Hunter recalled that it was around 8:00 or 9:00 in the morning and the two young men were preparing their breakfast. He said he was at their camp for only about a half hour. While Hunter was hitching his horse to the cart, Cummins unloaded some recently-gathered firewood from the cart and stacked it in a pile near their camp wagon. Hunter, in later testimony, testified that 12 days later when he visited the camp the wood was still in the same place where it had been unloaded by Cummins on the 4th of February. According to his testimony, when Hunter left their camp for Oakley he had to ride northeast the first couple of miles with no road until he got back to the junction of the road coming down from the Timbers and the road going north back towards Rock Creek. He stayed on that road past Buck Rice's place and on to Rock Creek and Oakley. The time of day that he was at the camp, as well as the time of his departure from the camp and other details of his visit became critical evidence in the upcoming trials surrounding the killing of the two men.[2]

Little did Ted Severe realize on that February day he was a witness to the beginning of one of the most bizarre and notable criminal cases in the history of Idaho. The case would go without resolution for the next six years and would become the subject of lingering questions, mythical stories, and misstated facts over the next 100 plus years.

---

2 Testimony at the Davis trial.

Present Day: The Site

Soon after moving to Idaho in 1968, I read several articles about the Diamondfield Jack story. The earliest I remember reading was written by Arthur Hart, a well-known, and highly regarded, Idaho historian and writer. He provided a vivid account of the cattlemen-sheepmen conflict in Cassia County during the 1890s, resulting in the killing of two young sheep herders, and the arrest of Jack Davis.

Not long after I settled in Idaho I visited the small city of Albion, where the trial was held in 1897. There, I stopped to read the historical sign located in the city park, which gives a brief account of the conflict and killing of the young men. The marker also gives a brief history of the trial and conviction of Jack Davis for those killings and of that town's role in the case. In the nearby Twin Falls area there is also evidence of Diamondfield Jack's influence, where his name graces bars and restaurants, doorways and walls.

My curiosity about the location of the shootings, in what was then Cassia County but is now Twin Falls County (having split off from Cassia in 1907), led me to ask a number of people in those areas if they knew where the shooting took place. The responses I received varied. If I was in the Burley-Oakley area, I would be told that it happened somewhere in the hills west of Oakley. If I asked the question in the Twin Falls area, I would be told that it happened someplace down in the South Hills towards Nevada; well to the west of where the Burley-Oakley people thought it happened.

The discrepancy, and the lack of seeming certainty about where this famous killing actually occurred stuck in my mind.

Over the next twenty-five years my curiosity and interest would be renewed each time some mention was made of Diamondfield Jack. For the most part my historical meanderings were directed to the history of the Civil War, but curiosity about Diamondfield lingered unsatisfied. Over the years I had occasionally driven into the general area both west of Oakley and south of Twin Falls, hoping to find something or someone that would give me further clues.

Years passed. Then, during a slow day at the 2009 legislative session, where I was serving as a state representative, I took a break and walked the ten blocks or so from the Statehouse to the Boise City Library. Stopping at the Special Collections and Documents Department, I asked if they might have any information on Jack "Diamondfield Jack" Davis. They retrieved a folder containing a small collection of newspaper articles that retold the general story about the case but didn't provide much new information.

One article, however, gave me the first real clue as to the actual location of the shooting.

Charles S. Walgamott, a historian from Twin Falls, wrote an article about Diamondfield Jack in the *Boise Capital News* dated March 3, 1938, entitled "Six Decades Back." In this article he gave a description of the killing as well as the location of the site. He outlined the history of the conflict between the sheepmen from the east side of the Cassia County area and the cattlemen to the west. He detailed the discovery of the two bodies and the reaction of the Oakley community upon learning of the boy's deaths. According to Walgamott, when the news reached the community, "the people in the affected country became aroused and seemed to be resting on arms. Rumors reached the cattle country around Rock Creek that an uprising of the east side would invade the cattle country with intention of destroying the entire population."[3]

Walgamott described the location:

"Two young men, Cummins and Wilson who were herding sheep, drove them in and established a camp between Goose Creek and Deep Creek, about six and one half miles southeast of where the town of Rogerson now stands, 28 miles south of the present town of Twin Falls, and some thousand feet west of Magic Hot Springs Road, where now can plainly be seen a loose rock monument, intended to show the location of their camp."

---

3 Six Decades back Quoted in Idaho Statesman March 7,1938

With this much information, I resumed my search to find the actual site. First, I bought a topographical map of the Rogerson area and started to familiarize myself with the area. I remembered my first trip to the region, which taught me that it is a big country and I would need much better and more detailed information before I could locate a particular spot there. Several months passed without my gaining much more information than what I learned from the newspaper article.

One day, while driving through Burley on my way to a meeting in Salt Lake City, the thought occurred to me that maybe the court records of the trial would have been preserved and moved to Burley, the current county seat of Cassia County. It was a high profile case at the time and certainly would have warranted preservation.

The young lady who helped me had never heard of Diamondfield Jack and had no idea how to search for records that far in the past. (To her, history was any time before she was born, some twenty years prior.) She was alone at the time, since the county clerk and the rest of the staff were off to a conference. She was as helpful as possible, but was somewhat new to the position and had not yet learned what historical records might be held in the courthouse. In any event, she was under the impression that all of the old records had been sent to the state historical archives in Boise.

That thought worked on my mind the rest of the trip, and as soon as I got back to Boise I went to the historical library to ask whether the Cassia County court records in fact had been transferred from Burley. I was advised that to their knowledge the records had not been transferred but instead still resided in Burley.

The search seemed to be at a standstill when I learned of Professor Phil Homan at Idaho State University, who had recently written a paper about Diamondfield Jack. I was able to contact Professor Homan and discuss his work, explaining that my interest in the case was mainly centered on finding the location of the site of the shooting south of Twin Falls. During our conversation he assured me that the historical society did have some records about the case. He had had a similar experience while searching for information both in Burley and at the State Archives, but eventually found that some limited information was indeed available.

I had become acquainted with Rod House, the State Archivist, during the 2009 legislative session, so I visited the center again, this time enlisting Rod's help. While Rod and I were going through a packet of information he had found, one of his staff members whom I knew came by. She asked what I was doing there, and I told her we were looking for information about Jack Davis but had not yet been able to find much. She said there was a fairly large box of information in storage and offered to retrieve it for us.

The "fairly large box" turned out to be legal papers of "Hawley James," and included his complete legal file on the Diamondfield Jack case, in which he served as defense attorney. This was equivalent to discovering the Comstock Mother Lode. In these legal papers I found the transcripts from the trial of Jack Davis and related legal actions involving Jeff Gray, as well as applications to the Board of Pardons, filings to the Idaho Supreme Court, petition to the United States Supreme Court, and many other transcripts and interviews of Hawley's, both in and out of court.

As I read the transcripts of the witnesses at the Davis trial, I started to narrow down the location of the camp wagon where the two herders were killed. With the assistance of two topographic maps, I thought I was able to identify landmarks on the maps that had been described in the testimonies. I thought I would then be able to go back down to the Rogerson area and find the spot.

Before returning to look for the site I was referred to Alex Kundle, a local rancher living near Duck Springs. Alex's family has owned a ranch near Duck Springs which had been referred to by a number of witnesses as being close to the site I was hoping to locate. Alex is very interested in history and is a member of the board of the Twin Falls Historical Society, so he was the ideal person to work with me. He has a great knowledge of the area and the local ranchers and how to get permission to go onto private property to explore and search.

I invited my friend and fellow legislator, Rich Wills, to make the trip with me. Rich is a retired Idaho State trooper with a natural instinct for investigation and exploration.

Rich and I met Alex at his home and laid out the maps and other information I had researched. I attempted to show Alex where the site was located based on the landmarks I had gleaned from newspapers and testimonies of some of the witnesses at Davis's trial. Being familiar with the area, Alex expressed his doubts about the landmarks which I had determined would mark the spot. When we drove up to the area it soon became clear to me that the landmarks on the map were different from those I thought the witnesses were describing. It became apparent that the passage of time between the on-site investigation by the sheriff and others, and their testimony at the trial a year later had evidently caused their memories to fade. It seemed their testimony about the directions of north, south, east, and west got a little mixed up. This fact became even clearer after reading and studying the testimony and viewing a map that Edward McClellan, a surveyor, had made at the time of Davis' trial. We did not have the success I had hoped for on our first trip to the site, other than familiarizing ourselves with the area.

Edward McClellan was a professional surveyor living in Elko County, Nevada at the time of Davis' trial. He had assisted in surveying much of Elko County and a few areas in Southern Idaho, and he had previously been hired by the Sparks-Harrell Cattle Company to survey around the Brown Ranch, Point Ranch, and Deep Creek Ranch, so he was quite familiar with the general area. At the time of Jack Davis' trial, McClellen was hired by James Hawley and John Sparks to make a map of the area showing the distances between the Brown Ranch and the site of the shooting, and then back to the Boars Nest Ranch. Davis and Gleason were known to have been at the Brown Ranch at sunup on the 4th and then were known to have been at the Boars Nest between 12:00 and 1:00 o'clock that same afternoon. One of McClellan's maps showed the air miles between the ranch houses at the Middle Stack Ranch, San Jacinto Ranch, the Boars Nest Ranch, the Brown Ranch, and the Point of the Mountain Ranch to the site of the shooting. Armed with these measurements from each of the ranch houses, it was possible to use a GPS and attempt to locate the site of the shooting.

With this possibility in mind, I thought of David Curtis as the go-to man to help with this project. David is a close friend with an adventurous streak who also happens to be an engineer by profession. Dave accepted the challenge.

Using Google Earth to find the search area we were looking for, he concluded we would have to make a trip to the area with his GPS to do the ground work and research. Assisted and accompanied again by Alex Kundle, along with his daughter, Melissa Kundle, we went to each of the locations—Middle Stack Ranch, San Jacinto Ranch, Boars Nest Ranch, the Brown Ranch, and the Point Ranch—and took readings with Dave's GPS, determining the coordinates of each location. We then went to the site we had determined to be the general area, hoping we could triangulate all of the coordinates to find the campsite where the shooting occurred.

We went to the middle of the field and used our first reading from the Point Ranch, which was 8¾ miles. At Dave's first reading he had to walk west a short distance to be 8¾ miles from the Point Ranch. His second reading was from the Boars Nest which was 21 miles and he was beyond 21 miles by a little more than a half mile. Dave had to walk south until he was 21 miles from the Boars Nest and then recheck the distance to the Point Ranch, which required him to walk east a short distance until he was again 8¾ miles from Point Ranch and still 21 miles from the Boars Nest. He followed the same procedure for each coordinate until he was able to bring the other two coordinates to a single spot.

At that point I told Dave and Alex that we had one more measurement to make as the final test. Charles Walgamott had written in his 1936 Boise Capital News article that the site was, "*some thousand feet west of the Magic Hot Springs road where now can plainly be seen a loose rock monument, intended to show the location of the wagon camp.*" We walked back over to where my car was parked on the Magic Hot Springs Road, and from the middle of the road Dave took a reading. We walked back to our spot where Dave's GPS had calculated the distances from the ranches and took the reading from the middle of the road. The distance was 1,035 feet.

The next question we wanted to answer was the reference by Walgamott to a loosely-stacked rock monument. A short distance from the spot we thought was the camp site, there is a small spring in a slight depression with a small ravine running through it. It was evident the ravine would carry runoff water from the higher ground as well as the spring water. Surrounding the spring are rocks stacked in a manner appearing to form four corners to the spring. It is obvious that the rocks had been stacked by someone for some reason. But if there was a purpose other than as a marker, or what may have happened to the rocks over the seventy years since Walgamott visited the area, no one will ever know. The stack of rocks is a curiosity, but it is evident that they were carried to the area and stacked. The rocks are not visible from the road and do not serve any purpose other than perhaps to mark a location of something.

These rocks are located near the camp site.

Believed to be the original rock monument at camp site. (photo by author)

After we located what we thought was the campsite, we looked around hoping to find something that would indicate a camp had in fact been here at some time in the past. We first found a piece of wood about nine inches long, three inches wide, and less than a half inch thick. It could have easily been part of a bow used to hold up the canvas top of a camp wagon. We found two old rusted-out tin cans, one of them a tobacco can.

One more clue came to our attention: A short distance to the north we saw a rocky butte. Was this the "butte" referred to by several witnesses during the trial? We thought so. As evidenced by the camp debris, and given the location near a butte, we concluded with relative certainty that we had located the campsite where the wagon was sitting that fateful day 115 years ago.

The Investigation I (1896)

When Noel Carlson reached Oakley late in the evening of February 16, 1896, word of the killings was sent on to Albion, the Cassia County seat, and to Sheriff Harvey L. Perkins. That information spread rapidly through the communities of Oakley and Albion, and men from both areas made the necessary preparations to travel back to the crime scene as rapidly as possible.

The majority of men from Oakley were sheep men and several of them had a personal interest in the death of the two herders. After hurried preparations, John J. Gray and F.M. Cummins left by 10:00 p.m. the evening of the 16th to return to the camp site. Gray was the owner of the sheep wagon and also owned one of the bands of sheep at the campsite. Cummins was the father-in-law of John J. Gray and the uncle of the deceased Daniel Cummins. The elder Cummins later testified that he himself was at the camp with Wilson up until the previous December when Daniel, his nephew, replaced him. Wilson and Cummins were herding not only Gray's sheep but also a small band of sheep that Wilson himself had been accumulating for the past several years.

The group from Oakley reached Davis Hunter's camp about noon the next morning; Gray was anxious to go over to the campsite to check on his sheep. The two Hunter brothers, Davis Hunter and Herman Hunter, accompanied Gray over to the campsite early in the afternoon of the 17th. Davis Hunter had already been to the site earlier in the day to gather some of the sheep that had scattered during the past 12 days. After gathering more of the sheep and examining the camp, they returned to Hunter's camp for the night.

That same morning while Davis and Gray were checking on the sheep, at about 6 a.m., Sheriff Harvey L. Perkins left Albion to return to Deep Creek and the site of the killings. He was accompanied by Dr. R.T. Story, a physician living in Albion, and several other concerned citizens from the area. They arrived at the camp of E. R. Dayley as darkness was settling in that evening. Ted Severe, the young man who had discovered the bodies, was one of two herders at Dayley's camp. After Hunter learned of the killings, he moved his camp closer to Dayley's; now both camps were only a couple miles northwest of the Wilson-Cummins camp.

The camp wagon was located left of center in clearing. (photo by author)

At sunup the next morning, February 18th, the men from both camps walked, or rode their horses the mile and a half or two miles over the hill to the site. The country surrounding the site was, and is, quite rough and hilly. Deep Creek runs toward the northwest through a canyon that in some places is narrow and steep. The hillsides are scattered with rocks and slashed by a number of deep ravines, making them difficult to traverse. The area around the camp is void of any trees but is covered with thick grasses and a scattering of sagebrush. The wagon was situated on higher and somewhat flatter ground, about 400 yards east of Deep Creek. The area where the camp was located was in a small basin with higher hills encircling the entire area, a mile and a half in the distance. Wilson's and Cummins' campsite had a good panoramic view of the area, making it an ideal location to graze a herd of sheep and be able to keep track of them.

Along with the Sheriff and Dr. Story, the other men who were present were Francis M. Cummins, John J. Gray, E. R. Daley, Charley G. Parkinson, Fred Wilson, Edgar "Ted" Severe, Davis, Heman (Herman?) Hunter, and Bert Lee. The sheriff and Dr. Story gathered physical evidence in and around the wagon; evidence that would become an important focal point during the trial that followed.

Sheriff Perkins described the site as they found it that morning:

"The wagon was covered, with projecting boards which extended out to make the wagon wider: the bed was cross-ways at the back end of the wagon with a small table that could be folded up against the wall in order to allow for a little more room to move around while not sitting at the table. Just inside the entrance or door way and on the right side is a small wood stove used for cooking and heating. The wagon is covered with a canvas cover with only canvas flaps hanging down over the entry way serving as doors to the wagon. The flaps were held open with strings tied to the bows. One flap was tied half way back and the other one was hanging down loose. The wagon faced the north and was located about 50 or 60 yards from the base of a knoll. Beyond the knoll was a ridge running from the north-east to the south-west which the group had to walk or ride over to reach the site."[4]

Two dead bodies were found lying on the bed at the rear of the wagon. The body of John Wilson was lying face down on the bed, his body covered over with either a blanket or his overcoat, and socks on his feet but no boots. Both men were clothed; Daniel Cummins was wearing an overcoat and Wilson was wearing pants and a long-sleeved shirt but no coat or jacket. A quick examination of the bodies revealed two wounds in Wilson's body and one bullet wound in the body of Cummins.

The two men appeared to have been preparing a meal at the time they were killed. There was a bread pan in the oven with partially baked bread in it, plus another pan of dough on the table ready to be put into the stove. Besides the usual eating utensils there were a lamp

---

4 Sheriff Perkin's testimony at the Davis trial.

and a book on the table. A corn-cob pipe was found lying under the front axle of the wagon about midway between the two front wheels. The stem of the pipe was missing, but the pipe appeared to be almost new, having been used perhaps only once or twice. The sheriff and Dr. R.T. Story concluded that the pipe likely belonged to whoever killed the two young men. Dr. Story testified he learned that the two boys did not smoke and he searched their pockets and around the wagon, and found no evidence of tobacco. Four empty cartridges were found near the rear wheel on the east side of the wagon. The shells were lying in somewhat of a straight line out from the wheel and were spaced about three feet apart. All of the empty shells were .44 caliber.

In addition to the three bullets that had killed the two young men, the sheriff found evidence that three additional bullets had been fired at the scene. A small hole through the covering of the wagon was determined to have been caused by a bullet. A fifth bullet was determined to have been shot down through the tongue of the wagon about even with the double tree and about 12 inches in front of the entrance to the wagon. The bullet penetrated through the wood and downward into a can of coal oil beneath the the tongue of the wagon. That bullet penetrated the coal oil can settling to the bottom without rupturing the bottom of the can. A sixth bullet had been shot through the right fender of a saddle which had been stretched over a sagebrush approximately two rods (30 feet) out in front of the camp wagon.

Both John J. Gray, the camp wagon owner, and E. R. Daley, owner of a nearby sheep camp, were questioned about the saddle and the fact that a bullet had penetrated the fender of the saddle. At the Davis trial, Daley was questioned about what made him think that the hole in the side of the saddle had been caused by a bullet. He explained it was the collected conclusion of five other men and himself it was caused by a bullet. He explained on the entrance hole the leather was pressed in and the leather was projected out on the other side. Daley explained the bullet penetrated clear through the saddle. When asked if he had examined the ground under the saddle Daley replied that they had not looked in the dirt under the saddle for the bullet.

Victim's monument located in Oakley cemetery. (photo by author)

Present Day: The Bullet

After finding what we thought was the site of the shooting, I reviewed some of the testimony of the witnesses trying to find some additional verification that we had located the correct site. While reading the testimony of E. R. Daley the thought occurred to me the bullet could possibly still be in the ground near the camp site.

A week later Alex and I returned to the area with metal detectors, hoping the find additional evidence to further verify the camp site. The two of us covered a large area around where we had staked out what we felt the camp site.

We again found items one would expect to be camp debris. Just below the ground surface we found a few rusty screws, nails, and a wagon bow clip. A bow clip is attached to the side of a wagon to hold the bow in place which forms the framework over which the canvas covering is stretched forming the camp wagon cover. We also located a few more rusted out tin cans in the same area where we had found the rusted cans the previous week. The two areas where we found these items were about ten feet apart and we conjectured that if the wagon had been placed between them it would have been reasonable that the cans could have been thrown out the front door to one side and the other items could have been worked on the other side of the wagon. From testimony we knew that the front of the wagon faced north towards a small knoll, the base of which, according to Sheriff Perkins, was approximately 60 yards from the wagon.

After satisfying ourselves where we thought the front of the wagon would have been, I stepped off 30 feet (the "two rods") from the front of the wagon to where the saddle was described to have been thrown over a sage brush. The area was at the edge of a flat rock formation resulting from a lava flow lying on the surface of the ground. The area is made up of small spots of soil and grass interspersed between patches of solid rock.

I started to use my metal detector at the edge of the rocks but still out in the dirt. Two or three feet towards the rock was a spot that was broken up where a lone sagebrush was growing up through the lava flow. The area around the sagebrush had two or three inches of soil and some grass growing amid the rocks. I could visualize a larger sagebrush, perhaps in this same spot a hundred years ago with a saddle spread over it, and I tried to imagine a bullet going through the saddle and into the ground behind it. I moved the metal detector around to the opposite side of the smaller sage brush and as I did the detector immediately sounded the familiar buzz indicating some metal under the ground. I knelt down with my probe to clear some dirt away to find what was under the soil.

As soon as I probed down I hit rock just an inch or so under the ground. I had to brush only a small amount of dirt away to reveal a lead bullet lying on the flat surface of the rock just barely covered by the dirt. I had anticipated and imagined in my mind the possibility of finding that bullet, but never thought I would be lucky enough to find it. It was a lead bullet flattened out slightly but definitely with the rings and markings of a bullet.

But was it *the* bullet? The next thing we had to do was to satisfy ourselves that the bullet *could* have been a bullet shot from one of the guns on that February day in 1896.

We talked first about the slim probability that the bullet would still be in the ground beneath where the saddle was, as described in court testimony 115 years earlier. The next question was whether this was a bullet of the period or whether it was fired from a gun more recently. The bullet would have lain in that spot for more than 115 years.

Alex and I decided that we needed to take the bullet to someone with ballistic expertise and get an opinion of its age. He knew an individual with such expertise and to him fell the task of verifying the bullet's age. Alex reported back that the bullet was definitely a bullet of the period.

Later, I took the bullet to John Taffin, the author of several books on revolvers and ammunition and recognized nationally as a gun expert. He explained that a bullet of the period would be solid lead as opposed to bullets produced after 1900, which are composed of additional alloys mixed with lead. The weight of this bullet is a little uncertain due to its having smashed into the rock, which may have removed some of thc lead. The bullet is flattened out but, in John's opinion most of the lead is there and it could be rounded back into its original shape and is a bullet made prior to the 1900s.

I also let Matt Perry, owner and gunsmith, of Buckhorn Gun Shop in Boise, examine it. Matt said that he believes firmly that it is a bullet of the period and in his judgment a .44 caliber.

In the best judgment of those who have examined the bullet, there is a high probability that this bullet is the one shot through the saddle on that fateful day in 1896 from James Bower's gun.[5]

With the passage of over 100 years, and with no eyewitnesses to reveal all the true facts, we will never know for certain the answers to all the questions raised by what we have been able to discover.

---

5 See picture of the bullet on page 88.

The Investigation II (1896)

The sheriff determined both of the bullets recovered at the site fit nicely in the four empty .44 caliber casings found on the ground at the rear of the wagon. Another bullet had been fired through the right fender of a saddle which had been laid over a sagebrush about 30 feet northeast from the front of the wagon.

The only gun found in or around the wagon was an older rifle. The investigators examined that rifle and found that it was not loaded and had not been fired since it had last been cleaned. F. M. Cummins, Daniel's uncle, testified he had cleaned the gun before he left the camp the previous December. Davis Hunter examined the gun and thought it was a Winchester 40-82, and he stated he did not find any shells for that gun in the wagon. Dr. Story said Cummins did have several cartridges in his pocket which did not fit the gun found in the wagon, but did not indicate the caliber. It is likely that those cartridges were for the gun that Hunter had taken back to Oakley with him in the cart back on the 4th of February. The rifle belonged to John Gray, the wagon owner.

In a newspaper article dated February 20, 1896, reporting on the murder, the Oakley newspaper, the *Oakley Sun,* reported that the only gun found in the wagon which would have been the only gun available to defend Cummins and Wilson was a "needle gun." Only two cartridges were found in the wagon for this gun, but even if the victims had been well armed they would have had no chance to defend themselves. The question was asked a couple of times at the trial, whether or not the old gun found in the wagon was a "needle gun." Testimony would indicate that the shells found in the wagon were two unfired bullets in Cummins' pocket, and they were for a later model rifle than a needle gun found in the wagon.

Dr. Story performed a post-mortem examination on the bodies of the two victims. The examination revealed that young Wilson had been shot twicc. The first bullet entered at the chin and traveled down though the shoulder, fracturing the number one rib and then going through the lung and lodging in the liver. The path of the bullet would indicate Wilson was either leaning over facing the shooter or, alternatively, the bullet was deflected by the chinbone and traveled on a downward path into the chest. The other gunshot wound entered Wilson's back an inch or so to the right of the spinal column and exited out the opposite side near his right breast. Cummins had one shot straight through his abdomen and out his back. The path of that bullet also indicated that Cummins was standing higher than the shooter, because it moved through the body at an upward angle.[6]

Daniel Cummings (left) and John Wilson. (photo courtesy, Idaho Historical Society)

On their way to the camp site, the sheriff and the doctor stopped at Rock Creek. They were concerned about finding enough local men to assemble a coroner's jury, the area being so sparsely populated at the time. As fate would have it, by the time Sheriff Perkins and Dr. Story arrived at the site, 15 or 16 men from Albion and Oakley had made the

6 Dr. Story's testimony during Davis's trial.

trip and were already gathered. That allowed the sheriff to form a coroner's jury and hold the inquest using the men present at the site.

The coroner's jury found the following verdict:

"Deep Creek, Cassia County, Idaho, and February 18, 1896.

We the coroner's jury found that Daniel Cummins met his death by a gunshot wound by a party or parties not known to us."

Signatures of the Jurors

E. R. Dailey, Foreman

J. J. Gray, *Bert Lee,*

Fred Wilson *F. M. Cummins*

Heman Hunter

The verdict was substantially the same for the death of John C. Wilson.

With as many men as there were combing the area, the sheriff had a problem keeping his investigation under control.

Later, when different pieces of evidence would be needed at trial, it became evident the men at the site thought particular items they had found would look nice on their mantels at home. Instead of being retained and secured by the sheriff, several key items had to be retrieved from individuals during the trial. The sheriff did not even keep in his possession the four empty cartridges which had been found on the ground near the rear wheel, nor the two bullets recovered from Wilson's body and the bullet recovered from the oil can under the wagon tongue. The sheriff had given the four empty cartridges plus the two spent bullets to Dr. Story. The doctor said he took them to his office and placed them in his showcase. Sadly, the showcase was not secured and the public had access to the exhibits. As a result, three of the empty cartridges and one of the two spent bullets were lost before the trial. Dr. Story told the court that his little girl told him she had taken items out of the show case and played with them at different times.[7]

7 Dr. Story's testimony during Davis' trial.

When the bodies of the two young men were returned to Oakley the community expressed sadness and anger, and a desire to avenge the boys' deaths. *The Oakley Sun,* reported the event on February 20, 1986, under the headline:

BRUTAL MURDER,

Two Sheepherders killed on Deep Creek, John C. Wilson was 23 years old and had been a resident of this place several years. His only crime was by industry and frugality he had acquired a few head of sheep and was pasturing them on government land. He leaves a brother and a sister to mourn his loss.

Daniel Cummins was the nephew of our well known citizen F. M. Cummins and his parents formerly resided here. His father currently lives at Walla Walla.

Taken altogether this was undoubtedly the most cowardly and brutal murder ever perpetrated in the State of Idaho.

Excitement has been at fever heat since the news of the murder had reached here. At the funeral of the two boys the speakers dwelt upon the high character of the young men and the foulness and brutality of the crime that had cut short their lives.

The people of Oakley and the surrounding area were in shock, and the citizens quickly rallied together, calling for swift punishment for whoever did the awful deed. The local newspaper continued to issue a cry for swift retribution and retaliation.

The feelings of the community are reflected in the verses that are etched on two granite monuments erected to their memory in the Oakley cemetery. Twin granite shafts about five feet tall, standing about three feet apart, appear as sentinels in the cemetery. Each marker has one of the young men's name and separate verses etched into the granite.

John C. Wilson

Died February 4, 1896

Age 25 yrs. 1 mo. 4 ds

Daniel C. Cummins

Died February 4,1896

Age 22yrs 3 mos. 23 ds

Assassinated while on duty.

Sadly in the early spring time.

Did we lay them down to rest.

Away from this cold unfeeling cline.

Safe away among the blessed

Death is certain the hour uncertain

Why did they kill them thus?

Pin on death's awful lance!

Why pluck the flower just in the budding

Why didn't they give the boys a chance?

VICTIMS of SHEEPMEN – CATTLEMEN'S CONFLICT

The local sheep men did not consider this incident to be just a random act by some crazed individual.

They were convinced that this was an act of vengeance perpetrated as a result of the ongoing conflict between the cattlemen and sheep men. As recently as two weeks prior there had been talk about a shooting incident in the same area where shots were fired into a sheep camp belonging to a local herder, Oliver Dunn. Speculation and suspicion began to surface immediately.

The finger of suspicion pointed to a cowboy by the name of Jackson Lee Davis.

Jack Davis was employed by the Sparks-Harrell Cattle Company in July of 1895 to work herding cattle in the Shoshone Basin, an area approximately 20 miles southwest of Oakley and 20 miles south of Twin Falls. The general superintendent of the Sparks-Harrell cattle operation, James E. Bower, hired Davis to ride herd on 450 purebred cattle on their prime summer range in Shoshone Basin. Bower was to play a prominent role as the case unfolded.

Most of the sheep owners in the Oakley area were quick to blame Davis and call for his arrest. Feelings among the sheepmen ran high against Davis largely because most of them had either experienced a personal confrontation with him or knew other sheep men in the area who had a run-in with Davis. They certainly had heard about the confrontation and shooting between a fellow herder by the name of William Tolman and Davis the previous November in the Shoshone Basin.

Jack Davis may have intended to keep his past a secret. His age and place of birth were listed differently several times over his life time. When committed to the Idaho State Penitentiary on February 27, 1899, his age was recorded as 28 years and 7 months and birthplace as West Virginia. This made 1871 the year of his birth. Yet his head stone listed his date of birth as 1863 and his birth place as New Jersey.

Jack Davis at 15. (photo, private collection)

His name—Jackson Lee—would strongly suggest a Virginia more than a New Jersey origin. In keeping with his reputation as a braggart and embellisher of facts, this raises the question of whether he adopted the name Jackson Lee Davis to bolster his own ego or elevate his image.

We know Jack worked in a silver mine in Silver City, Idaho during the summer of 1892. He later bragged about mining diamonds during the Idaho diamond rush during 1892-1893, in Diamond Basin southwest of Murphy.

Little is known about his stay in that area other than a letter from Frederic Irvin, his former employer at the Blackjack Mine at Silver City. In this letter, addressed to the Idaho Board of Pardons in July of 1901, Frederic and the mine foreman, J.B. Mattson, explained how Davis had been a good worker and had gotten along well with fellow employees. Both indicated they would hire Jack any time to work for them.

Before coming to the Rock Creek area, according to testimony Jack later gave before Governor Frank Steunenberg and the Board of Pardons, he had visited the Diamond Basin east of Silver City to search for diamonds during the 1892 diamond excitement. There had been talk of diamonds in the area since the early days of the Idaho territory. The newly appointed territorial governor, Caleb Lyons, became involved in a scheme of selling what were purported to be diamonds found in a diamond mine near the Snake River east of Silver City. After two years on the job Lyons suspiciously left Idaho with funds from the territorial treasury, leaving a lingering myth and a prospector's dream of a lost diamond mine. In December of 1892 diamond fever flared up again around Nampa, Idaho when a couple of locals claimed to have found the old diggings where Gov. Lyons had birthed his illusion of riches. Davis was working in Silver City at the time and made his attempt at prospecting for the elusive diamonds before appearing on the scene as a cowboy at Sparks-Harrell Cattle Ranch. After he spent a few days at the ranch talking about his search for diamonds, he was given the nickname Diamondfield Jack, an alias he carried to his death. A long-time employee at the ranch, William Trotter, is credited with giving Jack this enduring nickname.

Davis himself, in an appeal for pardon, testified before Governor Steunenberg and the other members of the Board of Pardons about how he had ended up in southern Idaho and northern Nevada working for the Sparks-Harrell Cattle Company.

He told them, "When that diamond excitement was on over here in 1893, I was working in Silver City in the Black Jack mine, and Fred Irwin was foreman, and the boys were all talking about the diamond excitement, and this San Juan excitement was going on, and I concluded I would quit the job and go down to the diamond fields. And I did go down there, but I didn't stay, I started to go down to the San Juan excitement and when I come to Rock Creek, Bill Trotter was there … and they asked me; did I ever work around horses; I says yes but I didn't come to break horses … Trotter asked me what my name was; I told him it was Jack; a fellow came up and asked him who that fellow was; he says, 'His name is Jack; he says; he came from the diamond fields; I guess we will call him Diamondfield Jack.' I don't think I had that name until 1895. I was not known in the Lamoille valley by that name at all; I never went under the alias of Diamondfield Jack."

Jack Davis in Goldfield, Nevada, 1905-07. (photo, courtesy Idaho Historical Society)

Letters to the Board of Pardons trace Jack's whereabouts from 1893 through July of 1895. He worked on several ranches near Wells, Nevada and the Lamoille Valley, located a few miles west of Wells. Davis's employers all referred to him as a good worker and again it was noted that he got along with his fellow workers. But Jack also earned a reputation of talking too much and was often accused of being a braggart and telling exaggerated and untrue stories.

The earliest record of Davis' whereabouts in southern Idaho is found in a letter written to the Board of Pardons in July 1901. Frederic Irvin confirmed that he and J. B. Mattson, foreman at the former Swift

Black Jack Mine and later foreman of the Sinker Tunnel located near Silver City, Owyhee County, Idaho, remembered Jack Davis quite well. They stated in their letter: "During the time he worked for us he gave good satisfaction; was a good miner and a pleasant man to get along with; we would have given him work at any subsequent time had he applied for it."

Jack was known to have worked for several ranchers in the Lamoille valley, located 15 or 20 miles west of Wells, Nevada, during the summer and winter of 1894 and 1895. This was before he was hired by James Bower to work for the Sparks- Harrell Cattle Company and ended up working near the Deadline Ridge.

Looking south from site of the shooting. (photo by author)

Looking west from site of the shooting. (photo by author)

The Dead Line Ridge

It was during the summer of 1895 that the cattlemen attempted to enforce their unilateral designation of a line referred to as "THE DEAD LINE RIDGE" separating the grazing rights of the cattlemen and those of the sheep men.

The ridge is located roughly 20 miles west of Oakley, running north to south and separating the Goose Creek drainage from the Shoshone Basin drainage. The Goose Creek drainage extends from the top of what is referred to as the South Mountains, approximately 20 miles southeast of the city of Twin Falls, south to northeast Nevada. The water collects into Goose Creek, which flows southerly into Nevada and then circles back into Idaho, flowing through Oakley and into the Snake River near Burley, Idaho. Water from the Shoshone Basin, which is on the west side of the Deadline Ridge, collects into Shoshone Creek flowing south into Nevada and into the Salmon Falls River, which then flows north into Idaho and on into the Snake River west of Buhl, Idaho. The cattlemen claimed the range land west of Dead Line Ridge and attempted to force the sheep men to remain east of the line.

The conflict seemed to flare up with more threats and counter threats when Jack Davis appeared on the range in July of 1895. That was about the time James E. Bower, the general superintendent for the Sparks-Harrell Cattle Company, hired him to work up in the basin.

Davis had been in the area for some time working at various jobs and had a good reputation for his work ethic. It was broadly believed by the sheep men that the cattle company retained Davis more as a hired gunman than to herd the purebred cattle.

The testimony of a number of the sheepherders at Davis's trial bears a noticeable pattern in descriptions of his method of bullying and intimidation. Davis, they said, would ride into a camp on an apparently friendly basis and ask the herder, for example, "Are you Sol Hale's men?" When the herder would answer in the negative, Davis would proceed to explain to the men that if they had been, they would have had a fight on their hands. Davis was always exhibiting his guns to add emphasis to the intimidation. One young herder testified that Davis would come into his camp frequently and eat with them, and even sleep overnight at their camp, but he would always deliver some intimidating message before he left their camp. He would approach the camp as a nice guy but then talk as a tough guy to herders about how he was going to kill some other sheep man not present.

Davis did follow through with one of his threats on a man named William Tolman in November 1895. Davis had on several occasions told other herders how he was going to shoot Bill Tolman if he ever ran into him. Tolman, carrying a rifle, came to Davis's camp and questioned him about making threats on his life. An argument resulted. When Tolman made a motion to get down off his horse, Jack pulled his gun and shot Tolman in the shoulder. This incident raised the ill feelings to a new level. Fearing retaliation or arrest, Jack Davis wisely decided to leave the area until things cooled off. Indeed, a warrant was issued for Jack's arrest on a charge of attempted murder. Davis left southern Idaho and drifted into Nevada, staying out of sight as much as he could. He reportedly remained in the Wells, Nevada, area living the good life offered to cowboys with money in their pocket, and waiting for the next job. He was also reported to have spent time visiting several ranches southwest of Wells in the Lamoille Valley, where he worked during the summers of 1894 and 1895.

Jack made no contact with any of the Sparks-Harrell outfits through the winter months until things seemed to settle down enough that he felt it was safe to return to the area. In late in January of 1896, he ventured from the Wells area further north to the H.D. Ranch. A day or two later he showed up at the Middle Stack Ranch with another Sparks-Harrell cowboy by the name of Fred Gleason. They seemed to be there without a cause or real reason, although Jack did testify later that the reason he was riding north into Idaho was to turn himself in to the sheriff over the shooting affair with Tolman. He and Gleason also talked about going out on the range to gather some of Spark-Harrell's horses but appeared to be in no hurry to go: The two spent most of one day while at the Middle Stack shooting at coyotes and some targets they had set up. When Davis ran out of .45 caliber ammunition, he reportedly borrowed some .44 shells from Gleason and continued shooting, using the .44 caliber shell in his .45 pistol. They appeared in no hurry to move on.

Since Davis had withdrawn from the range and was no longer issuing threats, the sheepmen became much more aggressive in moving further west towards the Salmon Falls River. One of their camps was southwest of the present town of Rogerson, about ten miles between the Point of the Mountain Ranch and the Brown Ranch.

The cattlemen were perhaps the real losers as a result of Davis's aggressive behavior. Davis had crossed the legal line and was now a fugitive from the law. With Davis out of the picture, at least temporarily, the sheepmen now had greater resolve to claim and occupy what they knew to be open public lands. During the next several months more bands of sheep moved westward, sometimes as close as a mile or two from the ranches belonging to the cattlemen. Some of the herders moved their sheep as far west as the Salmon Falls River, which is west and south of the present town of Rogerson, Idaho. The Rogerson area is 10 to 20 miles west of the Shoshone Basin, in the Deep Creek drainage.

At Davis's trial, T. M. Gray testified that one herder, James Dunn, allowed his sheep to graze so close to Gray's ranch that his sheep came down the lane to his home. Gray went out and warned the herder to keep the sheep farther back and away from his place.

Buck Rice testified that after being absent from his ranch for a few days, he returned to find sheep in his recently planted grain field and horses in his barn being fed with his hay. Rice said that he turned the horses loose and took the saddles up to his house. The next morning two men walked right past the house straight to the barn to retrieve their horses. Not finding them, they returned to the house to inquire about the disappearance of their saddles and horses. Rice told them that when he came home and found the horses in his barn, he turned them loose and brought the saddles up to his back porch. Rice said he wanted to see "what kind of men would use another man's hay and barn without permission."

Two other sheep camps had moved into the Deep Creek drainage a few miles west of Buck Rice's place near the Deep Creek Ranch. The movement of these camps elevated the concerns of the cattlemen and rumors began to circulate that the sheepmen were moving in and taking over the range.

Debris at the site. (Photo by author)

Around the 28th of January, 1896, Davis and Gleason moved farther north and were seen at the Boars Nest. While they were there, Harve Tranmer, who was living and working up at the Brown Ranch, told them he planned to ride up to the Point Ranch and on up to Rock Creek the next day or so. Both the Brown Ranch and the Point Ranch were over the Idaho border, the Brown Ranch on the Salmon Falls River about six or seven miles into Idaho, and the Point Ranch about 12 miles north of the Brown Ranch. Since Tranmer was riding as far north as Rock Creek, Gleason asked him to bring back a sorrel horse he had left at Henry Jones' place sometime earlier. Gleason said that Beady, the horse he wanted to retrieve, was the fastest horse in the outfit.

When Tranmer returned from Rock Creek to the Brown Ranch two days later he found Davis and Gleason had left the Boars Nest and were now at the Brown Ranch. Tranmer did bring the horse back with him and gave it to Gleason. Neither Davis nor Gleason indicated to Tranmer what they had been doing the two days they were at the Brown Ranch alone while he had been away, but it appeared they had been just eating and hanging out.

Called to testify as a witness at Davis's trial, Harve Tranmer offered his idea about what they might have done during those two days alone: He said they could have gone fishing, but he did not find any evidence of any fish having been caught. He said that about ten days after they left he found their fishing poles under one of their beds. In this case their "fishing poles" were a few sticks of "giant powder" (dynamite), which was the method of choice for fishing in those days. One blast of giant powder and the resulting concussion could turn up a goodly number of fish. Tranmer stated that he took the powder and stored it away in a wall of a rock barn. No further explanation was requested nor given. But just the mere mention of dynamite allowed William Borah, the prosecuting attorney at the Davis trial, to include in his summary that Davis had dynamite to use against Wilson and Cummings—even though neither Davis nor Gleason had taken the powder with them when they left the Brown Ranch the morning of the shooting.

On the 2nd of February, Davis and Gleason rode out from the ranch. They left without asking Tranmer to go with them or even telling him where they were going or why they were leaving. They rode east from the ranch at about 2:00 in the afternoon and did not return to the ranch until Tranmer was ready to go to bed. They told Tranmer that they did not find the horses they had gone out to hunt, and they asked him where they might find any horses. Tranmer replied he had no idea where any might be found.

Where they had been and what they were doing in the afternoon is not known but later it was determined that while they were riding back to the ranch, after dark they came upon a sheep camp belonging to Oliver Dunn. Dunn was camped east of the Brown Ranch and south of the Point Ranch. As Davis and Gleason were riding back towards the Brown Ranch they could hear a bell ringing off in the distance. Attaching a small bell on one of the horses was a practice enabling easier location of the horses in the dark. It was around 9:30 in the evening when the two riders heard the bell and as Gleason reported, Davis suddenly stopped and pulled his rifle out of his saddle scabbard and fired a round toward the sound of the bell. Gleason said as Davis continued to fire shots a series of shot were returned from what apparently was a sheep camp. Gleason said he rode off some distance away from Davis and did not participate in the exchange of fire.

Following the exchange of shots Davis and Gleason returned to the Brown Ranch and retired for the night, after a short conversation with Tranmer which did not include any mention of the shooting. The morning of February 3rd the two of them stayed at the ranch doing little else besides shoeing a horse and lounging around.

On the morning of the February 4th the two cowboys decided to leave the Brown Ranch and ride back upriver to the Middle Stack Ranch. Tranmer said that Davis and Gleason ate breakfast with him at about sunup and left shortly thereafter. In other testimony Tranmer wasn't certain if it was just daylight or sunup when the two rode away. The time of morning that they left the Brown Ranch remained controversial throughout the trial. The Brown Ranch was located in a canyon, where the time difference between daylight and sunup can be hours, particularly during the winter.

When they left the Brown Ranch they were trailing an extra horse and said they were going to ride upriver to the Middle Stack Ranch. But as they were about to leave, they made a curious inquiry. They asked if there was a place to cross over the river to the east side. They were told they could cross over upriver approximately two miles above the ranch. Since the Middle Stack Ranch and the Brown Ranch were on the same side of the river they then would have to cross back over the river when they got up to the Middle Stack Ranch. However, instead of going to the Middle Stack Ranch the men showed up at the Boars Nest Ranch, on the same side of the river as the Brown Ranch but across the border into Nevada. C.D. Edwards, an employee of Sparks-Harrell who was working at the Boars Nest Ranch, testified that, after eating dinner (lunch) at the San Jacinto Ranch three miles away, he returned to the Boars Nest, where he met Jack Davis and Fred Gleason coming out of the dining hall, having just finished their dinner. Edwards placed his return at one or two o'clock in the afternoon. He testified that Davis and Gleason had been there long enough to stable and feed their horses as well as to prepare and eat their meal. When he met them coming out of the dining hall he asked what time they arrived at the ranch and they estimated about 12:00 noon or a little before.

Edwards' testimony became an issue during Davis' trial because his estimate of the time of his return to the Boars Nest changed between Davis's preliminary hearing and his trial. At the preliminary hearing Edwards stated that he returned from the San Jacinto Ranch at around 3:00 o'clock in the afternoon, but at the trial he had reconsidered and said he believed it was closer to 1:00 o'clock. This testimony did not help the prosecution establish their case that Davis left the Brown Ranch early enough, as early as daylight as opposed to sunup, to ride up to Wilson's and Cumming's camp, commit the murders, and then arrive at the Boars Nest by early afternoon.

Thus daylight versus sunup, and being seen at the Boars Nest at about 1:00 o'clock rather than close to 3:00 o'clock, was important to the prosecution as well as the defense. Where they had been and what they had been doing between the time of leaving the Brown Ranch and the time they were seen at the Boars Nest became a center of controversy over the next several years. Both the defense and prosecution spent considerable time and money trying to prove either the impossibility or the possibility of making the ride from the Brown Ranch to the site of the shooting then on to the Boars Nest in the timeframe between their known presences at the two locations.

The total distance, on either of two practical routes, would be approximately 45 to 50 miles depending on how much cross country riding they may have done. It can be argued that the time saved by going a shorter distant off road would be offset by having to ride slower around rocks, and through ravines and snow drifts.

After leaving the Boars Nest, the two continued riding south and were seen at the Middle Stack Ranch at about 5:00 o'clock that same afternoon.

On the 6th of February they were at the H.D. Ranch where James Bower said he met them and then rode with them the 28 miles on to Wells, Nevada. Bower boarded the train to Reno to load some cattle to send to market. According to witnesses, Davis and Gleason remained in the Wells area for a number of days. They spent their time going from bar to bar, drinking and talking too much. C.B. Moore, the proprietor of a local hotel in Wells, testified that everybody up and down the river was talking about the killings. Moore commented the talk around town was that if Davis was ever caught, they would hang him.

Toward the middle of February, Davis was seen west of Wells in the small community of Crossroads in the Lamoille Valley, which is on the west slope of the Ruby Mountains. J.B. Gheen, proprietor of a small store at Crossroads, testified that during the winter of 1896 Jack Davis stopped at his store with a man named Randolph Streeter. Davis and

Streeter came into the store and Davis said he wanted to buy a drink of whiskey. Gheer told him that he couldn't sell him a single drink but he could sell him the whole bottle, which he bought. Davis paid with a twenty dollar gold coin. Gheen said he had known Jack Davis at various times when he worked in that section of the country several years earlier. "He owed me seven dollars balance on an old account," Gheen reported. Davis told Gheen to take the seven dollars that he owed on the account as well as the price of the whiskey. In the store at the time were two other men, Thomas Short and Al Dakin, sitting around the stove listening to Davis talk. Gheen testified, "Davis started to talk in a boastful fashion and was boasting about some shooting affairs he had up in Idaho where he had recently been working. I thought it was just some bragging cowboy talk as I often hear such talk in my store. I did not give any particular heed to what Davis was saying. I don't remember Davis mentioning the name of any individual person."

Frank Smith, a cowboy employed by the Sparks-Harrell Company, stated that on the 24th of February Davis told him he was going to leave the country because Gleason was getting drunk at Wells and blowing around about killing the sheepherders at Deep Creek.

After that, Davis was not heard from again until his arrest in Yuma, Arizona in March of 1897.

The local citizens in and around Oakley became convinced that "Diamondfield" Jack Davis was the perpetrator of the murders. The atmosphere in the area became hostile and the sheepmen soon demanded he be charged with murdering the two young men. When it was determined that Davis and Gleason were known to be together at the Brown Ranch on the morning of February 4, the finger of guilt pointed directly at Jack Davis.

The sheepmen of the community were quick to unite and come forth with a plan of action to find and punish the person or persons responsible for killing two of their own neighbors. Barely two weeks had passed before the Cassia County Wool Growers Association was organized; on March 7, 1896 the association met to approve a constitution which had been drawn up by member organizers. Article 2 of the Constitution stated:

"The object of this association is to provide means for the protection of life and property of all members of this association, to enforce all laws which are now or may hereafter be enacted for protection of life and property and to secure by lawful means the arrest conviction and punishment all persons violating such laws."

The minutes of this first meeting reflected rather strongly the real intent of the organization. Other than a motion to approve the proposed constitution, the only business in the meeting was a motion to offer a $1,000 reward for the apprehension and conviction of the parties that killed John Wilson and Daniel Cummins. Needless to say, the motion was carried.

A year later at their annual meeting, the minutes focused mainly on the Davis trial and expenses related to it. Their annual expense report listed $1622.45 in expenditures, $1,025.00 of which went towards paying either reward money or lawyers' fees in the Davis trial. The association hired Judge Orlando W. Powers of Salt Lake City to assist John C. Rogers, Cassia County prosecutor, in the Davis trial.

Prosecution attorney Orlando W. Powers of Salt Lake City was brought in to aid Borah. (Courtesy of Utah State Historical Society)

John G. Rogers, Cassia County prosecutor. (From French's *History of Idaho*)

The timing of the creation of this association reflects the emotionalism and bias of the times which had been steadily increasing due to the range war, and had culminated in the death of two young men. The community wanted swift retribution. It didn't take long for their focus to settle upon Jackson Lee Davis and his partner Fred Gleason. The sheepmen knew the guilty parties; they just needed to find them and go through the formalities of a trial.

Early in March 1896, Jack Davis and Fred Gleason were charged with the murder of John C. Wilson and Daniel C. Cummins. With the official charges in place, the manhunt began in earnest. Reward money for the capture of the two fugitives was quickly raised. The search was initiated for the two men and notices of a $5,000 reward for the arrest of Jack Davis, plus a $3,600 reward for the arrest and conviction of the party or parties who murdered John Wilson and Daniel Cummins, were sent to the surrounding states. There were a number of sightings reported to the sheriff by people thinking they had seen Davis or Gleason, but they proved to be look-alikes or someone only partially fitting the description of one or the other.

More than a year passed before Jack Davis and Fred Gleason were tracked down and arrested. Gleason was arrested in Deer Lodge, Montana in March 1897. Davis was caught the same month in Yuma, Arizona in a most convenient place for making an arrest: in the Yuma Arizona Territorial Prison. The fact that Davis was in prison just reinforced the belief that "Diamondfield" Jack was just a plain bad guy and must be guilty as charged. The Cassia County sheriff at the time of Davis' arrest was O. P. Anderson. He and two local sheepmen, J. J. Gray and E. R. Daley, made the trip to Yuma to return Davis to Idaho.

The Sheep Growers Association was very involved in this affair; the sheepmen, both individually and as an association, raised several thousand dollars of reward money for the arrest of Davis and Gleason. Following their separate arrests, both men were returned to Albion by the middle of March 1897 and both were arraigned for murdering Wilson and Cummings. Jack Davis was thought to be so guilty that his trial was set for just three weeks after his return to Albion.

Murderer or victim? (1897)

Following Davis's arrest, trial dates were set for both Davis and Gleason for the April 1897 court term in Albion. As soon as both the prosecuting and the defense teams were announced, the case assumed instant notoriety.

The Cassia County Prosecuting Attorney, John C. Rogers, quickly realized he would need additional legal assistance in order to manage both cases. William Borah, a special prosecutor from Boise, Idaho's capital city, was hired to assist. Borah already was well known as a lawyer in the capital city (He would go on to become Idaho's most powerful United States Senator, chairing the Foreign Relations Committee, earning a reputation as "The Lion of Idaho," and running for President of the United States in 1936). Another special prosecutor, Orlando W. Powers, was brought in from Salt Lake City to assist the county prosecutor. Powers was a well-known lawyer too, having been an associate justice in the Utah Territorial Court.

The prosecuting team proved effective in both detective work and handling of court procedures. As the trial got under way, the prevailing mood on both sides was one of war between the sheep interests and the cattle interests. The Wool Growers Association helped to finance the expense of special prosecutors, but most of the money was raised by the individual sheepmen from the area.

As expected, the cattlemen from the western side of the county put up money for the defense of Davis, most of it coming from John Sparks and Andrew Harrell, the Sparks-Harrell Cattle Company owners, and Davis' one-time employers. Since they had employed him during the summer and fall of 1895 they felt an obligation to defend him. Sparks and Harrell fulfilled their commitment by hiring the best criminal lawyers available in the states of Idaho and Nevada to defend Davis at his trial. The lead defense lawyer was James H. Hawley, also from Boise. Working with Hawley on the defense team were his law partner Will Pickett and a local lawyer from Albion, Kirkland I. Perky.

J.W. Dorsey, the attorney for the Sparks-Harrell company, worked with Hawley throughout the trial and the appeal process.

All four lawyers were well qualified. Hawley had gained a reputation as a hard-driving, skillful country lawyer. In 1878 he was elected district attorney and served in both houses in the territorial legislature. Later, he was elected Boise City Mayor from 1903-1905 and was elected for one term as governor of the state of Idaho from 1910-1911. In 1912, Perky was appointed to fill a vacancy in the U.S. Senate.

William E. Borah

James H. Hawley

(photographs, courtesy Idaho Historical Society)

Jack Davis's trial was scheduled to begin on April 6, 1897, with Gleason's trial to follow. The team of prosecutors set out to prove that Davis had been hired by the Sparks-Harrell Cattle Company to keep sheepherders from moving their sheep onto what the cattlemen considered their rangeland and, if necessary, to kill sheepherders.

"Diamondfield" Jack Davis, through his bullying actions and talking too much, was his own worst enemy. Davis was the type of individual who brought attention to himself by exaggerating and boasting, and as a result left a negative impression on most people he met. The characteristic most troublesome to the sheepmen was his constant bragging about past exploits and an air of intimidation he tried to impress them with as he rode the range. He would exaggerate the encounter from what may have been a verbal exchange into a shooting exchange, or at least he wanted to leave an impression that he had a shootout with someone up in Idaho. His story telling and boasting seriously damaged his credibility at trial.

By the time they were located, arrested, and returned to Albion, less than six weeks remained before their trial began. This left little time for the two sides to finalize their cases. Borah and his team of prosecutors did have an advantage since he had been hired to begin an investigation into the case soon after Davis and Gleason were charged with the murders back in March of 1896. Borah's involvement in the case began early enough that he was able to take the time to personally ride over the entire Sparks-Harrell operation in northern Nevada, interviewing potential witnesses and familiarizing himself with the territory. He also interviewed ranch hands on the ranches and developed a long list of potential witnesses. By April 5, 1897 the district attorney had a list of 61 witnesses who could be called to testify in the trial opening the next day.

By contrast, James Hawley was not hired until after Davis had been arrested and thus did not have as much time to do his investigation. Before the trial began, Hawley drove his carriage to Wells, Nevada and back up into Idaho to visit each of the Sparks ranches, interviewing as many witnesses as he could before the trial. The lack of time prevented him from properly developing two aspects of what should have been key to his defense. One, the timetable surrounding Davis's departure from the Brown Ranch and his appearance at the Boars Nest Ranch, and the other finding credible witnesses to properly tie together their stories and develop loopholes in the testimonies of the prosecution's witnesses.

Hawley soon learned that the prosecution was able to present generalized and circumstantial evidence to the jury which Hawley had not had time to research in order to build a rebuttal. The length of time it would take for a man to ride a horse from the Brown Ranch to the site of the shooting and then back to the Boars Nest was the one piece of critical evidence which could have been most damaging to the prosecution and most important to the defense of Davis.

Livery stable at Albion during Davis' trial. (restored newspaper photo by Joseph Larsen).

The Trial (1897)

The first of 16 witnesses who were called to testify was Sheriff Perkins. He established that on February 16, 1896 the bodies of John C. Wilson and Daniel C. Cummins were discovered in a sheep wagon located on a remote sheep camp in western Cassia County. The sheriff described the location of the wagon and its general construction features. He said the wagon faced north and was approximately 60 yards from the base of a bluff located just north of the wagon. The wagon was built with projecting boards which extended out to make the wagon wider in order for a bed to be placed cross-ways of the wagon bed at the rear of the wagon. The wagon was covered with canvas, giving it the appearance of a tent placed atop a wagon. Unlike later models, the camp wagon did not have a wood door built in; instead, the opening into the wagon was covered with two canvas flaps which could be tied back to open or tied down to close.

Sheriff Perkins testified that he and Doctor Story held an inquest on February 18; two spent .44 caliber bullets were recovered, one from the body of John Wilson, one from an oil can outside the wagon; and four empty cartridges were found at the scene.

Dr. Story next testified about the wounds each of the victims had received and made the conclusion, based on the evidence at the scene and the condition of the bodies, that they had been dead since the 4th of February, which was the last time they had been seen alive—when Davis Hunter visited the camp to pick up his cart. A series of witnesses was called to establish the fact that Jack Davis was in the area of northern Nevada at the end of January and as close as 16 miles from the site of the killings on the morning of February 4th.

Borah called several witnesses who spoke in generalities as to the speed at which a horse could travel over certain distances. It was said that a horse could travel at 10 miles per hour on fair to good roads. Borah was even able to make the assumption, and seemed to get away with it, that Davis and Gleason left the Brown Ranch at daylight rather than sunup, and that the two did not arrive at the Boars Nest until nearly 3:00 p.m. that same afternoon.

Three local residents (Thomas E. Harper, a local farmer not engaged in the cattle or the sheep businesses, Bert Lee and Charley G. Parkinson) were hired by the prosecution to return to the site of the shooting on April 8, two days after the trial commenced.

In Harper's words, "We were to examine the country in and about the alleged killing of Wilson and Cummings and about the Brown Ranch and those points." Harper and Lee both testified that it was about half a mile east from the point of killing to the road which leads directly to the Boars Nest. One witness testified it was only about 25 or 26 miles by horseback from the site of the shooting to the Boars Nest. The prosecution established the distance from the Brown Ranch to the site of the murder as 16 miles. A rider could potentially ride from the Brown Ranch to the point of killing in an hour and three quarters, and from the point of killing to the Boars Nest in two and half hours. Davis was purported to have left the Brown Ranch at sunlight and was seen at the Boars Nest by mid-afternoon, well within the time frame the prosecution wanted the jury to believe was possible.

This critical piece of evidence was left in the minds of the jury despite the testimony of a surveyor, Edward C. McClellan, interestingly employed by the defense team but called to testify on behalf of the prosecution. The first and most obvious contradiction was McClellan's calculation of 37 3/4 "*air miles*" as opposed to Harper's 36 to 41 "*over-the-road miles*." Considering the hills and turns in the roads, the over-the-road miles from the Brown Ranch to the site of the shooting and then on to the Boars Nest would have to be substantially longer. Harper and Lee had testified the road miles would be a distance of about 16 miles from the Brown Ranch to the site of the killings and from 20 to 25 miles from the site of the shooting to the Boars nest, for a total distance of between 36 and 41 miles. However, McClellen's put the road distances between those points at 48 and 54 miles, depending on possible short cuts. These points were made by the prosecution within a very generalized context and Hawley did not have enough factual evidence to counter or develop his own argument, as he later attempted to do in his appeal for a new trial. That appeal was made to District Judge Stockslager, who refused to grant it. Hawley eventually appealed to the Idaho Supreme Court.

Based on the decision of the Idaho Supreme Court on June 15, 1898 in reference to Hawley's appeal for a new trial on Davis's behalf, it would have been incumbent on Hawley to have developed and used in Davis's trial the factual evidence and improbability of Davis being able to ride a horse over the terrain and distance from the Brown Ranch to the site of the killing and then to the Boars Nest within the timeframe well established by credible witnesses. The Supreme Court's decision read, in part:

"NEW TRIAL-WHEN SHOULD NOT BE GRANTED- A new trial should not be granted on the ground of newly discovered evidence where such evidence is merely cumulative, or where it was within the power of the defense, by the use of reasonable diligence, to have produced such evidence at the trial."[8]

Borah skillfully brought one witness after another and established Davis's motive by calling attention to his threats and actions while riding the range near Deadline Ridge. He made threats of killing sheepmen, and Wilson was a sheep owner. Davis had boasted to several different individuals in Nevada that he was involved in a shooting incident with some sheepherders up in Idaho, and those individuals were called as witnesses. Witnesses described Davis and Gleason as being armed with both a Winchester rifle and a six shooter, and stated they were shooting at coyotes and doing target practice at the Middle Stack Ranch for a good part of a day. The witnesses further described how Davis ran out of .45 shells for his gun, borrowed some . 44's from Gleason and was shooting them in his .45 caliber six-shooter.

William Trotter, a longtime employee of the Sparks-Harrell Cattle Company, gave testimony that Davis had traded coats with Frank Smith while at the Middle Stack Ranch, explaining that the coat he was wearing was too light in color and could be seen at night. The coat Frank Smith had was a darker coat and not as visible in the dark. Testimony later indicated that upon Davis's return from the Brown Ranch to the Middle Stack Ranch he traded the coat back to Smith. This testimony was never directly connected for any reason other than to further establish a premeditated devious motive by Davis. The connection for Davis wanting a darker coat did play out on the night of

---

8 Supreme Court decision June 15, 1898, *State vs Davis*.

February 2nd near the Point Ranch. The prosecuting team very effectively established and connected this incident as evidence of deliberately carrying their intent to kill sheepherders. The jury, made up largely of sheepmen, could easily connect the killing of Wilson and Cummins in their camp with the shooting at the Oliver Dunn camp just two days before the February 4th shooting.

Two brothers, Loren Wilson and Joseph Wilson, testified they were inside the Dunn camp wagon when they heard rifle shots apparently being aimed towards their camp. They got outside their camp wagon with their rifles and determined they were being fired upon. They could see flashes of light from the shots in the darkness and responded by shooting back toward the flashes. Loren, during his testimony stated he felt like he was the first to shoot at what he thought was a lone man shooting at their animals. The horses were hobbled with bells attached approximately 300 hundred years away from their camp wagon. It was after Loren's shots, directed at the man, that the figure turned his shots towards the two herders. Loren estimated eight or nine shots were exchanged before the person doing the shooting retreated and ceased firing. The attack resulted in one of the Wilson's horses being shot and killed.

Throughout the trial the prosecution introduced circumstantial evidence at best. Borah and the prosecution successfully established to the jurors that a crime had indeed been committed, and that Davis was at least near the location at the time the crime occurred. They put together a mosaic pattern of evidence including an array of witnesses which, when threaded together, certainly pointed the finger of guilt toward Diamondfield Jack.

William Tolman was brought to the witness stand and instructed he could not mention the fact that Davis had shot him in the shoulder. All he was allowed to say was that he and Davis had had a little trouble. Everyone on the jury knew exactly what the trouble had been. The jurors were presented a picture of a man certainly capable of committing the crime he was being tried for.

Hawley and the defense team objected numerous times but were overruled nearly every time. They called a few witnesses trying to prove it would not be possible to have ridden a horse the distance required and be back to the Boars Nest within the two-to-four-hour timeframe. But their arguments did not prove convincing. The jurors, mostly sheepmen and a few cattlemen from the community that had lost two of their own, did not take long to reach their decision—a decision based on the reputation which Davis himself had created, as well as the skillfully-woven circumstantial evidence presented by the prosecution. In their minds, Jack Davis was most assuredly guilty as charged.

On April 15, 1897, the Boise, Idaho *Statesman* carried the story about the verdict in the trial sent in by their correspondent. It read, in part:

The jury made up its mind in two hours. An anxious audience had scarcely cleared the courtroom when the bailiff notified Judge Stockslager that the jury had reached a verdict. Back came the crowd, back in filed the solemn jury. Up from his cell came Diamondfield Jack. The jury foreman announced to the Judge, "We find Jack Davis guilty of murder in the first degree."

Nine days later Judge C. O. Stockslager sentenced Jack Davis to be hanged by the neck until dead. The execution was set to happen on June 4, 1897. Jack was to be housed in the Cassia County jail during the appeal process.

James Hawley was surprised and disappointed in the verdict. He immediately gave notice that he would file for a new trial. Perhaps the most telling fact, though, is this: Fred Gleason's trial was held later in April, in the same court for the same crime and using the same evidence, but the jury acquitted him.

Other voices have expressed similar doubts.

Verlaine L. Powell, an accomplished author and historian from Albion, Idaho, wrote and produced a one-act play about the trial of Diamondfield Jack. The play is performed by the Albion Valley Players during their community summer celebrations. There is a line in the play, somewhat profound, where the narrator states, *"It appeared as though the concept of reasonable doubt had given way to reasonable possibility as justification for conviction."*[9]

The verdict in the trial continued to be discussed. Charles S. Mark, Editor and Publisher of the *Albion Times*, wrote to the Board of Pardons on June 7, 1901, some four years later:

---

9 Verlene L. Powell's One act play " The Trial".

Albion, Idaho, June 7, 1901

"TO THE HONORABLE BOARD OF PARDONS,"

Boise City, Idaho

Gentlemen: one of the first pieces of job work I did in coming to Albion three years ago was a transcribe in the Diamondfield Jack Davis case. In doing that work I was compelled to read all the evidence pertaining to the case three times. Before coming to Albion all I knew about was what I had read in the newspapers, which was not favorable to Davis by any means. But after reading all the evidence and discussing it with others, I came to the conclusion that there was something outside of mere evidence to convict that man, because, in my opinion, there is not the slightest "circumstantial" to say nothing about "direct" evidence in all the evidence upon which to convict a man.

When I aired my opinions regarding the unjust decision of the jury before the public I soon found out to my complete satisfaction that "evidence" had nothing at all to do with the verdict, public opinion at that time being so strongly against Davis that the jury would very likely have been mobbed had they acquitted Davis.

Very respectfully yours,

(signed)

C. S. Mark

Diamondfield Jack Davis's ordeal was far from over and his notoriety was just beginning.

James Hawley's work was also just beginning and would continue over the next five and a half years. As expected, Hawley filed for a new trial within weeks and Davis knew that he would not be hung on the appointed day. In the following years Diamondfield Jack Davis would sit in his cell and seven times experience the anxiety, and then the relief, of having a judge or governor delay and reset the date of his execution.

Following the motion to Judge Stockslager for a new trial, Hawley had the time to begin finding witnesses who could counter some of the circumstantial evidence which had convicted his client. During the summer of 1897 he spent a lot of time further developing his motion for a new trial. He studied the trial transcripts and formulated his reasons and justifications for filing the motion.As Hawley perfected his argument he submitted to Judge Stockslager his briefs in which he listed some 15 points or errors and 12 sub-set errors which he felt had occurred during the original trial. Among the salient points listed:

- Error in that the evidence fails to show that defendant was present at the time of killing of the deceased or at the time deceased received his mortal wounds.
- That the evidence shows that defendant could not have been in the place of killing on February 4, 1896.
- That the evidence fails to show the guilt of defendant beyond a reasonable doubt, or shows his guilt at all.

Also included in Hawley's presentation to Judge Stockslager for a new trial were a large number of affidavits written before notaries public, sworn to be true, about differing testimony which had not been given, or that could have been given, during the trial which would have raised some doubt in the prosecution's case. A number of other affidavits were also obtained and submitted in Hawley's appeal. One such affidavit was submitted by an Andrew D. Gray, brother to Jeff D. Gray, wherein he swore that on the morning of February 4, the morning of the shooting, he was on the range south of the Brown Ranch and had noticed two riders, one trailing an extra horse, fitting the description of Davis and Gleason riding on the road west of the Salmon Falls River. West of Salmon Falls River would be the side which Jack and Fred testified they had traveled on their way to the Bore's Nest Ranch.

Hawley's team produced a couple of statements they felt were prejudicial and biased remarks by jurors both before and after the trial. One sworn statement by Mary A. Gordon stated that she, in the company of her daughter, heard George W. Gray, a juror on Davis's trial, make the statement before the trial that "Diamondfield" Jack Davis was guilty of killing Wilson and Cummins.

On September 6, 1897, Kirkland I. Perky, the lawyer from Albion who served on Hawley's defense team, wrote a letter to J.C. Rogers, Cassia County attorney and the prosecuting attorney in the Davis trial, inviting him to join together and hopefully put to rest the question regarding the improbability of Davis and Gleason having been able to make the ride from the Brown Ranch and around to the Boars Nest. In the letter he stated their request:

The roads are now in better condition than at any time of the year, and range horses are in better condition than in the winter or spring. While a test now would if successful from the prosecution's standpoint, not necessarily show that the same ride could be made in February or April, still if it is determined that the ride could not be made now, it would necessarily follow that Davis and Gleason could not have made it February 4th, 1896, and so could not be guilty of the murder of Wilson and Cummins.

We therefore propose as follows: That you select two or three men, proficient riders and thoroughly acquainted with the section of the country to be ridden over, and mounted upon first class range horses in good conditions, and start the men from the Brown ranch at a given time, have them ride to the point of killing over any route they may desire, and deem shortest and swiftest, stay at said point from five minutes to one half hour, or one hour, as prosecution deem proper and best, and thence ride to the Boars Nest ranch over any route they may think easiest and swiftest, keeping careful record of the time of arrival, and the time spent at the point of killing.

J.C. Rogers did not reply to Perky's invitation for nearly three months. On December 4, 1897, Rodgers replied by letter to the invitation; his response reads, in part:

"This paper is wholly outside of all forms or rules relating to criminal causes and I presume, was not sent in the nature of a legal document and will not be answered in that light but as public prosecutor. I will communicate to you a statement which you may use in connection with your statement if you wish to.

In the first place, it must have been apparent to the defendant and his counsel long prior to the trial of this cause that that would be his defense, if it was a bona fide defense, and the proper time for the defendant and his counsel, knowing his life was in jeopardy, to have made this communication was before the jury had passed upon the proposition and decided that he was there at the time of the killing.

Since the jury has passed upon this question of fact, it being one of the controverted facts in the case and the only defense which the defendant interposes, it is no longer a matter for the consideration of the courts and is practically an immaterial matter to the State. We have in view of what we consider wholly unreasonable affidavits upon part of defendant as to ride, filed some affidavits with reference to this matter but have at all times considered it, since the jury has passed upon it, as settled."

This reply from Rogers did not preclude the defense from using this new evidence before the Board of Pardons nor from presenting individual letters along with lists of local residents who had signed petitions expressing their current positions as to Davis's guilt.

Lewis H. Sweetser from Albion expressed his personal conviction of the innocence of Jack Davis by stating

It is my opinion, which is shared by many of the citizens of this county that heard all the evidence in this case, that the evidence was entirely insufficient to justify the verdict of guilty of murder. The evidence was purely circumstantial and not at all strong either against Gleason or Davis. The evidence against Gleason was practically the same as against Davis yet the former was cleared. It is true that Davis was shown to have a very unsavory reputation and it appears to me that the jury must have allowed his reputation to bias their judgment. But bad as his character may have been I honestly believe him innocent of the murder of Wilson and Cummins. My desire to see Davis treated with justice is my sole reason for making a plea in his favor.[10]

On January 12, 1898 Judge Stockslager overruled the motion for a new trial. The judge's refusal to grant a new trial was not good news for Davis, but was not unexpected by Hawley, who was prepared to go to the next level with an appeal to the state Supreme Court.

Six days later, on the 18th of January, Hawley filed his appeal to the Idaho Supreme Court over the denial for a new trial, using basically the same facts he had previously used in his motion to Judge Stockslager. He included in the appeal several procedural issues. One such issue,

10 Foot note Letter from Lewis H. Sweeter.

which Hawley felt was very pertinent to showing the jury's bias, was the affidavit signed by Mary A. Gordon, wherein she stated that George W. Gray, a juror on the trial of Jack Davis, said while in her home before the trial that "Jack Davis and James Bower were the parties that killed the two sheepmen on February 4, 1896. He made this statement in the presence of my daughter, Addie Gordon, and did not qualify or modify his statement at all."

Hawley had been busy since the April trial gathering affidavits and new evidence. He and Puckett renewed their efforts to obtain new evidence and favorable testimony. In early spring Hawley sent several letters to individuals in Idaho and Nevada, requesting affidavits from them giving evidence as to the character of Jack Davis while he lived, socialize,d or worked for or near them in the past. Before Hawley appeared before the high court, he and Puckett accumulated numerous letters, petitions, and affidavits which they used in their argument.

The Supreme Court studied the case for several months and handed down its decision on June 16, 1898. The Supreme Court upheld the lower court's decision in refusing to grant Davis a new trial. This decision suddenly turned the case from one of high hopes and expectation for a reversal in Davis's favor to a new fear that the sentence to be hung might become a reality. Hawley immediately sent a petition back to the Supreme Court for a rehearing, claiming some new points or evidence.[11]

The Idaho Statesmen reported the latest setback in its July 29, 1898 edition with this headline:

HIS LAST HOPE VANISHES

Rehearing in the Davis Murder Case Denied

ONLY BOARD OF PARDONS LEFT

Little Likelihood of an appeal to the United States Supreme Court—Text of the Last Decision

The Supreme Court has denied the petition for a rehearing in the case of "Diamondfield" Jack Davis, who is under sentence to hang in Cassia County for the murder of Wilson and Cummings, the sheepherders. The Supreme Court decided the original appeal some time ago, but a motion for a rehearing was presented which it was

11 Supreme Court Decision June 15, 1898 [53 Pac 678].

claimed presented some new points. The Supreme Court in denying the motion says:

The petition for rehearing although quite voluminous presents nothing new. No questions arising upon the evidence or the law applicable thereto which have not heretofore been fully considered and passed upon appear in the petition, and as we have already expended much time in a careful and laborious examination of the record and the briefs of counsel in this case we are confident that a repetition of our labors would serve no other purpose than delay.

A new trial should never be granted on the ground of newly discovered evidence when such evidence is merely cumulative, nor when the alleged newly discovered evidence was easily within reach of the defendant, and could, with reasonable diligence, have been produced at the trial. To grant a new trial on such grounds would not be subservient to the public good, but would on the other hand, encourage a careless and loose presentation by the defendant of his defense.

By this decision the last hope of Davis so far as the courts of Idaho are concerned vanishes. It was said the case would be taken to the United States Supreme Court, but that is not likely. The Board of Pardons is the only power that stands between Davis and the hangman.

With both Judge Stockslager's denial in January and the Supreme Court's unfavorable rulings in June and July, Hawley's available options were narrowing. Often the Board of Pardons is viewed as the last resort but Hawley felt that the Board of Pardons had the constitutional powers to grant pardons, which is in essence the power to overturn decisions of the Supreme Court as well.

The Board of Pardons I (1898)

The Idaho Constitution, Article IV, section 7, created the board of pardons:

The Governor, Secretary of State, and Attorney General, shall constitute a Board to be known as the Board of Pardons. Said Board, or a majority thereof, shall have power to remit fines and forfeitures, and to grant commutations and pardons after conviction and judgment, either absolutely or upon such conditions as they may impose in all cases of offenses against the State, except treason or conviction on impeachment. The Legislature shall by law prescribe the sessions of said board and the manner in which application shall be made, and regulate proceeding thereon; but no fine or forfeiture shall be remitted, and no commutation or pardon granted, except by the decision of a majority of said board, after a full hearing in open session, and until previous notice of the time and place of such hearing and the release applied for, shall have been given by publication in some newspaper of general circulation at least once a week for four weeks

The pardons board would turn out to be the most important element in Jack Davis's fight for his life over the next four years. An examination of the *Record of the Board of Pardons* for the years of 1898- 1920 reveals that the board held more hearings or reviews concerning "Diamondfield" Jack Davis than any other inmate in the Idaho prison system. From 1890-1920 the Board of Pardons heard 1,147 cases, of which two cases had nine recorded actions taken by the board, two having seven actions, and one with six actions. All of the other cases required one to five actions by the board to either grant or reject the request for a pardon. In the case of "Diamondfield" Jack, the Board recorded twenty-three separate actions from July 25, 1898, the date of Davis's first application for a pardon, to December 17, 1902, the date of his pardon.

Hawley felt that he had new compelling evidence, coupled with a changing public opinion across Cassia County as to Jack Davis' guilt, to appeal to the Board of Pardons for a full pardon. His application to pardon Davis was submitted to the Idaho Board of Pardons on July 25, 1898. The board agreed to an October 1898 hearing to review the application, which included trial transcripts, affidavits, depositions, and a number of petitions completed and signed by citizens from Oakley, Rock Creek, and Albion and forwarded to the board. These petitions stated that the signers now believed that Davis was unjustly convicted.

An editorial in Albion's newspaper, *The General News*, dated September 17, 1898, expressed doubt as to the guilt of "Diamondfield" Jack. The editorial said, *"No one has ever claimed that they saw him do it, and it has not even been proven that he was, at the time of the murder, where it was committed. And a man is never guilty until he is proven so."* It was clear that public opinion had shifted.

During the spring and summer of 1898 Hawley and his defense team had been busy searching for new evidence and obtaining new collaborating testimonies which would help convince the board of Davis's innocence. The most important evidence that Hawley's team worked on was establishing the impossibility of Davis and Gleason being able to leave the Brown Ranch near sunup, which would have been near 9:00 in the morning, and then be at the Boars Nest by 12:00 to 1:00 that same afternoon. Hawley engaged several different riders to make the trip from the Brown Ranch to the site of the killing and on to the Boars Nest. The results convinced the defense team of the improbability of Davis and Gleason being able to make the ride within the necessary timeframe. After the initial trial, the importance of the alleged ride became paramount in Hawley's appeal.

Hawley spent a considerable amount of effort obtaining affidavits from J.B. Gheen, a businessman from Lamoille Valley, Nevada, who had become fairly well acquainted with Davis during the summer of 1894 and 1895 when Davis worked for at least three different ranchers in the area. Mr. Gheen wrote several letters in response to requests from Hawley concerning the character of Jack Davis while he was working in the Lamoille Valley area. These letters countered the testimony of a young man by the name of Randolph Streeter, the 18-year-old son of Emily Hayward and stepson of J.D. Hayward, who had signed an affidavit for the prosecution strongly implying that Davis had admitted, in his presence, killing the two sheepherders in Idaho. Gheen obtained affidavits from Randolph himself, along with his mother and stepfather, stating Davis did not make any statements mentioning specific names of people he killed but spoke only of a shooting incident, which referred only to the shooting of a sheepherder in the shoulder and shooting into a sheep camp at night.

Along with Streeter and his parents, Gheen obtained signatures and affidavits from several other local residents in his area who also heard Davis boast about being involved in a shooting in Idaho, never mentioning the names of the two victims, Wilson and Cummins. Other affidavits indicated Davis had been a good employee and got along well with the employees he worked around.

On September 12, 1898, the Supreme Court re-sentenced Davis to be hung on October 31, 1898.

During the October hearing before the Board of Pardons Hawley laid out an array of new evidence and affidavits. The announcement which startled not only the board but the entire hearing room was Hawley's assertion that it was James E. Bower and Jeffrey D. Gray, and not "Diamondfield" Jack Davis, who had killed the two herders. The *Idaho Statesman,* dated October 18, 1898, reported the dramatic development this way:

SENSATIONAL DISCLOSURES

At the opening of the afternoon session Mr. Hawley read the affidavits showing that Cummins and Wilson were killed by Jeff Gray in self-defense. It was evident the members of the board had some intimation they were coming, for no surprise was depicted on the countenance of any of the members. A number of corroborative affidavits were read before the main affidavit was presented.

After reciting the fact that Bower was in the employ of Sparks-Harrell Cattle Company at the time of the killing, the affidavit states that Bower had business in Reno, and left Rock Creek about 9 o'clock in the morning of February 4th for the Nevada town. He wore a heavy fur coat and carried a revolver, which hung in a scabbard from his left shoulder under his under coat.

On October 22nd Governor Steunenberg granted Davis a reprieve until December 16, pending the hearing on the application of pardon.

The members of the board, Governor Frank Steunenberg, Secretary of State George J. Lewis, and Attorney General R.E. McFarland, made the decision to continue the hearings in December in order to study the new evidence being introduced by Hawley.

Forty-two years later the *Idaho Statesman* wrote a series of articles on the Diamondfield Jack Davis case. A few of the facts of the case were given a little different slant than the original reporting. The 1938 version of the reaction of the board following the confessions of Bower and Gray before the Board of Pardons reads a little differently than the 1898 version of the story:

That was a surprise!

The Pardon Board went momentarily dizzy. The state rocked. It was a mess. Everyone was in a high state of dither except Diamondfield Jack secure from the hubbub and gaining weight in Cassia County jail. Jeff Gray and James Bower confessed both slayings. They popped up with a long fascinating statement to prove just how guilty they were. The Board of Pardons listened to the tale with some feeling that the leg of justice was being pulled. Never the less some ground was found for doubt. So many chaps were going around boasting about doing murder that the Board grants itself, as much as the defendant time to cogitate. Diamondfield Jack's request for pardon was continued to December 1. Governor Steunenberg granted a reprieve until December 16.

With the confessions, it now appeared both Bower and Gray had falsely testified, under oath, at the Jack Davis trial, and some doubt began to surface in the minds of the board members. Governor Steunenberg remarked that he considered it a fatal defect in Bower's affidavit that he had testified in the trial differently than he had testified in the affidavit. He also said, with regard to Streeter's conflicting affidavits, that he did not know whether he would believe either one of them. Reverting again to Bower's affidavit he repeated his former statement in a little different form, adding that Bower stood in the light of a perjurer.

During the December hearings the feeling was evident that perhaps some kind of game was being played in an attempt to free Davis. Hawley could sense this feeling so he was prompted to address the board in an attempt to alleviate that impression. Hawley said, "I feel under the circumstances, that it is incumbent upon me to make a statement of this kind. I understand that there is a doubt, either from the evidence itself or from the statements of others, or in the minds of the gentlemen representing the Sheep Growers' or Wool Growers' Association, or their attorneys, about the bona fideness of this matter; that it has been urged or at least argued that instead of this application being made in good faith, that it is an attempt to hoodwink and deceive this Board; that persons, in order to save the life of another, have seen fit to perjure themselves in regard to this affair, and I desire to say and pledge my honor both as a man and as an attorney, that I cannot, in the light of correspondence I have had and the efforts that I have made, culminating in this matter, imagine for a moment that I have been deceived."[12]

The board didn't know quite what to do with this development. They did not believe Davis when he declared his innocence and now they didn't believe Bower's and Gray's story either. They had convened their October meeting to consider Jack Davis's petition for a pardon but the meeting turned from Davis to the confessions of two other men who had confessed to the killing of the two men which Davis had been tried and convicted of murdering.

As reported by the *Statesman*, October 21,1898:

The board realizing the importance and gravity of this case, as well as the importance of their action, both as affecting the defendant and the public, desire a most thorough investigation, and an opportunity for all persons interested to be heard. The affidavits last referred to were filed upon the day of the hearing and no opportunity has been had to inquire into their correctness. Counsel for the defendant has also referred to us a number of the other citizens whom they allege have been informed in regard to the killing by Gray.

Believing therefore delay is necessary to fully ascertain the truth of these matters, we have passed the resolution of continuance above set.

These events naturally turned everyone's attention to the Bower and Gray story. Were they in fact involved in the shootings or were they somehow part of a conspiracy to free Davis? Whatever the case, the

12 Hawley papers.

Board of Pardons was faced with a dilemma. They still had the Davis appeal to deal with, but at the same time they could not ignore the Bower and Gray confessions.

The residents of Cassia County now had to deal with a turnabout. What had been a strong certainty by the community of the guilt of Jack Davis had now become an uncertainty, due to the unexpected surprise revelation that two of their own neighbors, and not a notorious bad guy from the outside, had admitted to the killing of Wilson and Cummins.

This new information surprised the entire Cassia County citizenry. The question now centered on what effect all this new information would have on the Board of Pardons as they deliberated their decision. Would they believe the Bower and Gray story?

The Burley Bulletin carried an obituary on February 16, 1922, entitled

AN EARLY PIONEER PASSES.

J. E. Bower died in Long Beach, California Thursday February 9 at the age of 68. The death came as a surprise and shock to his many friends in this community as he and Mrs. Bower had gone to the California city but a few months ago to spend the winter.

The remains arrived in Burley on Tuesday accompanied by Mrs. Bower and their daughter and grand-daughter. Funeral services were held Wednesday morning in the Elks hall under the auspices of the local Elks lodge, of which organization Mr. Bower was a charter member. The high respect in which the deceased was held was evidenced by the large attendance at the services and the profusion of beautiful floral offerings.

Following the services the body was taken to Artesian City, where it was laid beside that of a little daughter who passed away at Albion some twenty years ago. It was Mr. Bower's request that he be buried at Artesian City, his old ranch home.

Mr. Bower was one of the first settlers in Cassia County. He came here in the fall of 1873, and located on the ranch at what is now Artesian City in 1877. He made his home there with his estimable wife for many years, living in Albion during the winter for a time to send

their children to school, then returning to the farm to manage their herds of cattle and look after other property. Mr. Bower was a quiet unassuming gentleman, but was considered one of the substantial builders among the early pioneers and businessman of ability by the later generation.

James E. Bower was a man with a history of accomplishments. He was a strong community supporter which earned him the respect of his community, as noted in his obituary. But at least one of his life experiences left him with memories of regret and sadness. In the absence of diaries, the only reliable source of information and facts are public records. In the case of Mr. James Bower, public records provide some very detailed and important information about his life.

Bower was born in Allen County, Ohio, on February 1, 1854. When he was still an infant his parents moved to Chillicothe, Missouri, where they homesteaded a place of their own along with other folks from surrounding states, both above and below the Mason-Dixon Line. His early education was mainly gained in the local schools in and around Chillicothe, but he was sent back to Ohio where he lived with an aunt while attending some school. James grew up learning the art of farming and stock raising, which remained his lifetime occupation.

As a young boy he experienced a country at war until he was eleven years old. When the Civil War started, loyalties were mixed between the northern sympathizers and southern sympathizers. As a result, a number of gang-type organizations were roaming through the Missouri countryside, fighting for neither side but plundering and robbing the citizens at will. These groups were referred to as "bushwhackers" and neither local law enforcement nor the military had the extra manpower to eliminate them. It was said of some groups that they would ride into a community or even onto a farm and demand that a meal be prepared for them—but before they would eat, they would make the cook eat the meal first, just in case it had been poisoned. Despite the courtesy of a free meal, the bushwhackers would often help themselves to whatever else they desired. As a boy growing up, young James must have witnessed some of these raids and experienced the fear within the community when the thugs rode into town.

By the time James was 15 he was venturing out into the world on his own. In 1869 he left home and went across the plains to Wyoming, moving a herd of cattle to that territory. From this experience and from this point forth in his life he became a cowboy and spent the majority of his life on cattle ranches. James did try to work in the mines for a short time before showing up in Idaho in 1872 to work for cattleman A. Jasper Harrell.

Jasper Harrell was nicknamed "Barley" Harrell, supposedly because of the sack of barley he always carried behind his saddle to provide grain for his horse.

Jasper arrived in northeast Nevada from California where he had developed his cattle operation. He moved his operation into Nevada due to severe drought conditions in California, arriving in Nevada at a most opportune time. The population in California was growing rapidly the demand for beef cattle was expanding, and the completion of the transcontinental railroad through northern Nevada allowed rapid shipments to that growing market.

These events opened the opportunity for a large-scale beef operation, and the right man to take advantage of the opportunity was Jasper Harrell. He searched the entire northern Nevada territory and made the decision to settle in the northeastern section. According to Joseph A. Young's book, *Cattle in the Cold Desert,* Jasper Harrell made his first land purchase in the Thousand Springs Valley in 1870, then bought a herd of cattle in Texas and trailed them into northern Nevada to begin his operation. Harrell immediately began to expand his holdings to the east, along Goose Creek toward the Utah border, establishing the Rancho Grande and Wine Cup ranches, and to the west along Salmon Falls, forming the western edge of his operation. Harrell claimed the rights to the water from the springs, creeks, and meadowlands throughout the region. He also continued to buy more and more cattle to put on his expanding land claims and acquisitions. As his holdings expanded, his need for new rangeland likewise expanded. He rode the range of northeastern Nevada and south central Idaho as a true frontier figure, always with a lever action rifle in a saddle scabbard and a six-shooter in his holster. He paid his range crews every three or four months with gold and silver coins which he carried in his saddlebags. He timed his arrival at the cow camps for dinner. After dinner, Harrell would gamble with the crew and usually win back a large portion of the wages he had just paid them.

As the summer heat dried out vegetation in the lower country, Jasper Harrell sent his foreman, James Bower, further north across the Idaho border to look for suitable summer range at higher elevations. It was during one of these explorations near Goat Springs, approximately 17 miles southwest of Rock Creek, that Bower climbed to the top of a high ridge, looked out to the north and for the first time saw the Snake River Valley. He rode down into the valley and while there met two gentlemen from the Rock Creek area: Arthur D. Norton and Miles G. Robinson. These two men were among the first to bring cattle to the western part of Cassia County in 1871. They spoke highly of the area and pointed out the potential of the vast rangelands. When Bower went back to report his discovery of thousands of acres of potential new grazing land, Jasper Harrell immediately started to buy more Texas cattle and move them north onto the vacant land. He soon established ranches on Upper Goose Creek, Rock Creek, and along Salmon Falls Creek on the Idaho side of the border.

Between 1870 and 1881 Jasper Harrell built an empire that was reported to be one of the largest cattle operations in the United States. The recently-completed railroad opened markets from San Francisco to Chicago, which allowed Jasper to market his product at the highest prices available.

Harrell began to sell his ranching operation to John Sparks and John Tinnin in 1881. In June of 1883 it was reported that Harrell had sold the remainder of his operation to Sparks and Tinnin. This sale included 30,000 head of cattle and a large number of horses. It also included meadowland and rangeland said to be 100 miles square. In November of 1883 the *Elko Independent* printed an article calling Sparks and Tinnin "the cattle kings of the West." They were running 70,000 head of cattle and the 17,000 calves they branded annually made them "one of the largest ranchers in the West."

While James Bower was working for Harrell north of the border in Idaho he made the decision to homestead a place of his own. One of Harrell's northern ranches called the Shoe Sole Ranch extended into Idaho to within a few miles of the little settlement of Rock Creek, Idaho. In 1873, other than a few scattered ranches in south central Idaho, the only community of any size in the region was Rock Creek, an Oregon Trail stop. Shortly after the transcontinental railroad was completed a major freight depot and stage line were established at Kelton, Utah. A road, passing near Rock Creek, was established from the newly completed station at Kelton to Boise and on to Portland and Seattle. Because of its strategic location, Kelton saw large amounts of freight unloaded from trains and hauled to the northwest by wagon. Rock Creek became one of the main stops for the teamsters transporting freight and passengers to and from the north. But in the early 1880s the Oregon Short Line was completed across Southern Idaho eliminating the freight and passenger traffic from Kelton and Rock Creek. This left Rock Creek to be a center of cattle ranching in western Cassia County and eastern Owyhee County.

Just north of Harrell's Shoe Sole Ranch and nine miles southeast of Rock Creek, Bower settled on a small creek called Dry Creek. Bower developed a prosperous cattle operation of his own. In addition to the clear cool water running out of the hills south of his spread he drilled an artesian well on his property which produced warm water. Over the years the warmed water was not only used for swimming but also to irrigate early spring crops giving them a couple weeks' earlier start. The area later was known as Artesian City as Bower supported a school and a church there.

Bower and Gray (1898)

James Bower's employment with Jasper Harrell's cattle company in northern Nevada and southern Idaho marked the real origin of the Jackson Lee Davis story.

Jefferson (Jeff) Gray, a 27-year-old cowboy, would play a pivotal role in the chain of events which changed both his life and that of James Bower. Even less personal history about Jeff Gray has survived the years, although he still has relatives living in the section of country where the "Diamondfield" Jack event occurred. The Gray family was very helpful and willing to share what little of the history and information about Jeff has survived.

Jefferson Gray was born into a large family of eleven brothers and sisters in Bitterroot County, Montana, in 1869. Approximately 1876, Thomas McBeth Gray and Susan Adams Gray moved their family to Marsh Creek, Idaho. After about a year in Marsh Creek, which is now known as Albion, they moved the 30 miles to Rock Creek. The family then moved into the Salmon Falls River area which is about 35 miles southwest of Rock Creek. There, Jeff's father settled and established his own cattle ranch near the Salmon Falls River. The area where the Gray's ranch was located is now called Grays Landing and for the most part is under water in the back waters of Salmon Falls Reservoir.

Gray grew up working with cattle and around ranching. He had at one time worked for the Sparks-Harrell cattle operation and in the winter of 1896, was working for his brother-law Henry Jones, who was married to his sister Wilmoth. Gray not only worked with the cattle but spent considerable time with the horses belonging to the ranch.

Jeff moved to southern California to live with a sister soon after 1900. There is very little information available about him during his stay in California. The 1920 U.S. Census indicates that he was living in a hotel in Los Angeles for the winter and listed his occupation as a miner. We do know he died in 1922 in Death Valley, California at the age of 53.[13]

Jeff Gray (seated; other man unknown). (photo courtesy Sally Jones collection)

On February 4, 1896, James Bower woke to a chilly midwinter morning prepared to continue his trip to Reno. He had traveled the

13 Information about Jeff Gray provided by Sally Jones.

night before from his home ranch on Dry Creek about nine miles to the Shoe Sole Ranch near Rock Creek. The previous day had been warm enough to thaw the ground slightly and since a light snow had fallen during the night, the road would be not only soft, but a little muddy. Over the next three days Bower was going to have to ride his saddle horse over 100 miles to catch a train at Wells, Nevada; he had to be in Reno by the 6th or 7th to make arrangements for a shipment of cattle from Reno to the eastern market. Bower was about halfway through a journey he began in Ogden, Utah on January 29, hoping to return to Ogden several days before his step-daughter's wedding on February 10. The journey from Ogden required a 92- mile train ride to Kelton, Utah, then from Kelton, an 85-mile stagecoach ride to Oakley, Idaho and then nine or ten miles onto his ranch at Dry Creek.

Bower had to return to his ranch at Dry Creek, Idaho, to attend to his stock, which were located at his ranch as well as on Sparks' Shoe Sole Ranch near Rock Creek, about nine miles away. He also had personal business to take care of at the county seat at Albion, which was about 35 miles from his ranch. Bower was the superintendent over the series of ranches belonging to the Sparks-Harrell Cattle Company, ranches ranging from Wells, Nevada northward into Idaho as far north as Rock Creek.

The Sparks-Harrell Cattle Company had an important lawsuit pending at Elko, Nevada which had been set for a hearing on February 12. The witnesses for the company were working on the ranches along the Salmon Falls River near the Idaho-Nevada border. It was Bower's responsibility to get the company's witnesses to the trial on time. He also had to be in Reno on the 6th or 7th of February to ship the cattle. Another reason for this trip was to try to obtain the necessary legal papers to complete the adoption of a step-daughter before her marriage, which was planned for February 10th in Ogden. Mrs. Bower and her husband earnestly desired that Eva be adopted by Mr. Bower in order for her to be married by his surname. They were under the impression that in order to accomplish this he would have to do it in Idaho at the courthouse in Albion, the county seat.

Albion was a 35-mile trip from his ranch. Bower made the trip on January 31st, but after consulting with attorney K.I. Perky, Esq., Bower was informed that owing to Eva's absence from Albion, he could not secure the adoption papers there, but could secure them in Ogden, just as well as at Albion. It wasn't necessarily bad news, but Bower would have preferred to avoid the 70-mile round trip on horseback from his ranch to Albion, only to learn that the adoption matter could be settled in Ogden.

After completing his personal business at his ranch, Bower was finally ready to head south towards Wells, Nevada and the ranches along the way. He would need to make stops at the Point Ranch, the Brown Ranch, the Boars Nest Ranch, the San Jacinto Ranch, and the Middle Stack Ranch, all along Salmon Falls River, to advise certain of their employees to be in Elko for the trial. After spending the night at the Shoe Sole Ranch he stopped at the Rock Creek store for a few minutes. While at the store Bower purchased a new corn cob pipe and some tobacco before continuing on his journey.

Prior to reaching the store, Bower had noticed a lone rider going over the hill on the road leading from Rock Creek. After his stop at the store, the rider had gotten ahead of him some distance but was still visible when he rode over a rise in the road. A couple miles past Rock Creek, Bower was overtaken by Jeff Gray, who was currently working for the Jones brothers in the Rock Creek area. Bower and Gray had known each other for several years, since Gray had worked for the Sparks-Harrell Company in the past and Bower was the general superintendent of the Sparks-Harrell operation, which meant that Jeff would have worked directly under Bower at some point. Gray was on his way to Buck Rice's ranch. He had made arrangements to meet Buck Rice there so the two of them could go out on the desert to round up some horses from the winter range.

As the two rode along, one topic of their discussion focused on the conflict between the sheepmen and cattlemen, which seemed to be increasing. Bower pointed out to Gray the lone rider a mile or so ahead of them. They could see the man briefly as he rode over a rise in the road. Bower expressed his curiosity about who he might be and where he might be riding. For the past several months a man by the name of Bill Vale had been going from one ranch to another with no apparent purpose other than visiting, and suspicions were floated that Vale was spying for the sheepmen. There were rumors that an organized movement was under way for sheepmen to move into the area and take the country over, and Bower wondered if that rider might be Vale. The sheepmen had been moving their herds further west from the Oakley and Goose Creek ranges and some rumors were circulating about herds coming down from north of the Snake River. The cattlemen, having been on the range for a number of years before the sheepherders arrived, were of the opinion that they had priority rights over the sheepmen. But legally there was nothing giving them any special rights, so the sheepmen felt they had equal rights to the open public ranges.

Gray explained to Bower that he was on his way to Buck Rice's place as the had made plans to go out to the winter range and round up some horses belonging to Henry Jones, his employer. Since fewer working horses were needed during the winter months most ranchers would turn their horses out to graze on the open range rather than use more expensive feed to sustain them through the winter months. Buck Rice owned a ranch approximately 20 miles southwest from Rock Creek where he grew grain and hay for his animals. He also owned a place some 16 miles west of his home place, which he referred to as his "desert place." Buck was in the business of raising horses and overseeing the winter grazing of his horses as well as horses belonging to other local ranchers. His desert place was near the winter rangeland and had a cabin and corrals. Buck and others would start rounding up the horses, putting them in Buck's corrals until they could be sent back to the individual ranches.

As Bower and Gray rode south toward Bower's destination, the Point Ranch, and Gray's destination, Buck Rice's place, they came to a place called Goat Springs. A man riding in a two-wheeled cart approached them from the south and later reported that Bower and Gray parted to both sides of the road without having any conversation with him as he passed. Bower knew the man was a sheepman since he would have recognized any cattleman from the area. Bower and Gray later learned his name was Davis Hunter, and that he had just come from the sheep camp of John Wilson and Daniel Cummins. Bower and Gray estimated the time of meeting Mr. Hunter to be 10 or 11 o'clock in the morning.

A short distance past the point where they met the two-wheeled cart, they came to the fork in the road at the top of Goat Springs Hill. The road to the right went southwest to the Point Ranch and the other road continued south to Buck Rice's place. At that point Bower made the decision to ride on to Buck's place with Gray and have dinner (the midday meal, now commonly called "lunch") before continuing on to the Point Ranch. The real reason Bower wanted to stay on the road they were on was his curiosity about the man in the two-wheeled cart as well as the lone rider they had observed riding ahead of them. Who were they and where was the one going and from where did the man in the cart come?

Buck Rice's place was another two or three miles down the road from Goat Springs and they could see the tracks of the cart on the road as they approached the lane that led up to Rice's house. It was about a half mile from the gate up to Rice's house and barns. Since there were no tracks in the light snow covering the lane to the house and no smoke coming from the chimney, it was evident Rice was not home. They then decided to continue on the same road and on to the Point Ranch, figuring it would be the same distance as if they returned to the fork in the road.

The road from Rice's place continued south for a couple of miles toward Soldier Creek. Just past Soldier Creek the road angled eastward towards the Shoshone Basin and up to a place called "The Timbers." The hills south of Twin Falls are referred to as the South Hills and, with the exception of a few square miles on the tops of the hills, few trees around there grew large enough to be cut and used for lumber. Despite the lack of a forest of pine trees, the whole area had a beauty and fascination of its own. Then as now, the area called "The Timbers" is located about ten miles east of Soldier Creek along Shoshone Creek, which runs south into Nevada and into the Salmon Falls River.

For several miles along Shoshone Creek an unusual stand of large timber grows. The ranches throughout the region depended on this timber for the lumber to build their cabins and barns. The stand of trees is even more picturesque because of the absence of any trees in the rest of the basin, with its vast expanses of prairie grasses and sagebrush. This is the area the cattlemen considered some of their prime summer and fall grazing land.

After they rode past Soldier Creek, Bower and Gray both testified that they left the road they had been on, still following the cart tracks which angled off to the south and went up a hill. If they had remained on the road it would intersect with the road coming down from the Timbers and Shoshone Basin. Cutting across they would still intersect the Timbers road a mile west from where they would have been if they had continued following the road. Their decision to leave the road and ride cross country was prompted not only by the fact that it would cut some distance from their ride but also because they were also able to follow the tracks of the two-wheeled cart that had aroused Bower's interest. He wanted to know where it had come from and more importantly, whether the rider was Billy Vale. Even though Bower and Gray had lost the tracks of the rider they suspected to be Billy Vale some place back around Goat Springs, Bower wanted to determine not only where the cart had come from, but where Vale may have been heading.

Davis Hunter testified at Jeff Gray's trial that the man Bower thought was Billy Vale was actually a man by the name of Jess Wilson. Hunter had passed Wilson, who was riding back to the Dunn camp from Oakley, traveling about a mile ahead of Bower and Gray. He and Hunter had a brief conversation at the fork in the road near Goat Springs.

Jess Wilson had, in fact, taken the fork in the road at the top of the hill and was heading back to an area south of the Point Ranch. Wilson worked for a sheep owner named James Dunn who was currently grazing his sheep northeast of the Brown Ranch and a mile and a half south of the Point Ranch. The Dunn camp was the sheep camp that Jack Davis and Fred Gleason shot into on the evening of February 2, killing a horse. Jess Wilson was the brother of Loren Wilson and Joseph Wilson, the two herders who were at the camp the night of the shooting.

Bower and Gray both testified how they cut across the countryside until they reached the top of the hill where they intersected the Shoshone Basin or Timbers Road and could look down toward Deep Creek. From there, they could see two sheep camps off in the distance to the south. They described the closer of the two as being located on the east side of the creek and the other as being about three-fourths of a mile west of the first camp and located on the opposite, or west, side of Deep Creek. They testified that upon seeing the camps they rode down to the nearest one, which was the camp located on the east side of the creek. That camp was the one belonging to John Wilson and Daniel Cummins.

It was noon when the two riders, Bower and Gray, arrived at the camp. Wilson and Cummins were preparing their dinner (lunch) and they invited Bower and Gray into the wagon, and engaged them in conversation. Bower said he was smoking his new corn cob pipe, purchased that morning at the Rock Creek store, as he climbed up into the wagon. The pipe became an important piece of evidence in the later trial.

According to Bower's testimony, at some point in the conversation he asked Wilson, who seemed to be the spokesperson, what they were doing in this part of the country.

Wilson then asked Bower who he was and Bower introduced himself as the superintendent of the Sparks-Harrell Cattle Company.

According to Bower, Wilson replied, "Yes, I know you" or "I have heard of you."

Bower then asked if they thought it right for them to come over onto the cattle country.

Wilson replied, "We have just as much business here as you have."

Bower said, "I don't think you do and you don't pay any taxes over here so you don't belong over here." Bower was under the impression that they had come from north of the Snake River and were rumored to be coming into the country to take it over.

"We do pay taxes over here," Wilson replied. Bower said he thought he was lying and he thought they were tramp herders. Wilson jumped to his feet and said, "You are a lying son-of-a-bitch" and as Bower jumped to his feet, Wilson either grabbed him by the throat or hit Bower, and the two of them fell to the floor of the wagon with Wilson on top of Bower.

Gray either jumped or was pushed out of the wagon onto the ground. When he stood up he could see the two men struggling with each other, Bower on his back and Wilson half standing, half kneeling over Bower. Gray said he immediately pulled his gun. Bower was clearly disadvantaged, with his body hanging part way out of the wagon and his back lying across the dash board or end gate. Bower wore a shoulder holster with a .44 caliber pistol under his overcoat and he was attempting to pull the gun out. Gray was standing outside the wagon, watching the struggle, when suddenly he saw Cummins standing behind the two with a rifle in his hands, saying something like he was going to shoot the two of them. Gray said he thought Cummins was pointing the gun at him so he shot at Cummins.

B.P. Howells, the Prosecuting Attorney, asked Gray, "Did Cummins fall down or drop?" Gray replied that Cummins dropped the gun and may have staggered back against the wagon but he did not fall. When the sheriff investigated the scene he concluded that the gun Cummins was holding was not loaded nor had it been fired since it had been cleaned some time earlier.

When asked what he did next, Gray replied that when he looked down at Bower it looked like Wilson had forced Bower's gun from him and was about to shoot. Gray stated he was sure Wilson had the gun in both hands and was cursing something about "fixing the two of us." Gray said he shot at Wilson but thought he might have missed because Wilson didn't seem to let go of Bower. Gray said he thought Bower was dazed because he didn't seem to be fighting back.

Gray was standing only three or four feet from the two men, and he fired another shot at Wilson.

The first shot had hit Wilson in the back, just left of his backbone, and the bullet exited just to the right of his right nipple.

The second shot hit Wilson in the chin and the bullet traveled into his chest, breaking the first rib, and continued through the lung, lodging in the liver. The second shot caused Wilson to relax his hold and fall partly across Bower. Bower said he tried to get up but couldn't lift Wilson off until Gray got up into the wagon and helped him.

Bower and Gray testified that as they were helping Wilson off the floor and up onto the bed; Wilson said he thought he was badly hurt, but Bower told him he didn't think he was hurt that badly. They both thought Cummins acted as if he was just scared and not hurt at all. During the shooting and confusion, their horses had spooked and run off a short distance from the wagon. Bower walked out towards the horses which were about 50 or 75 feet away from where they had left them. As he returned with the horses he said Gray was outside the wagon working with his six-shooter and was either taking cartridges out or putting some into his pistol. Gray stated in testimony that he had fired only three shots; Bower stated he did not remember firing any shots from his gun. He maintained that when he carried a pistol he generally kept the hammer chamber empty. When questioned later in the trial Bower admitted that the chamber could have had a shell in it and may have fired, but he did not remember it happening.

The testimony of the sheriff, J.J. Gray, Dr. Story, and E.R. Dayley clearly identified that at least six shots had been fired around the camp wagon. Sheriff Perkins and Dr. Story testified that two bullets had hit Wilson and one bullet entered the body of Cummins. One bullet had pierced the covering on the wagon and another bullet had penetrated through a hound, which is a part of the tongue of the wagon, and into a coal oil can which had been placed under the tongue. That bullet had settled to the bottom of the can and was recovered and used as evidence. A sixth bullet had been shot through the fender of a saddle which had been placed over a sagebrush approximately two rods (30 feet) in front of the wagon.

At a later time in a trial, Gray was questioned about whether or not he had heard shots fired from Bower's gun. Gray said he felt certain that at least one and possibly two shots had been fired from Bower's gun. Gray was further questioned as to whether or not one of the shots he thought had been fired from Bower's gun had gone through the tongue. Gray replied that it very likely could have been the bullet.

Bower and Gray left the camp soon after retrieving their horses. Bower said he thought they should ride over to the other sheep camp to let them know what had happened. Gray said it would be a bad idea because he thought they would just get into more trouble. They continued down the draw towards Deep Creek for a couple miles to the point where the road from the Timbers crossed through Deep Creek. Bower had considerable blood on his coat as a result of Wilson lying across him when he received the wound in the chin. The two of them stopped at the creek crossing so Bower could clean himself up and wash the blood from his coat and hands.

It was at Deep Creek that Gray made the decision to return to Rock Creek and Bower decided to continue on to the Point Ranch. Bower told Gray that what had happened was a very serious thing and he warned him to be careful riding back to Rock Creek. Bower rode on to the Point Ranch where his brother–in-law, I.T. Robinson was the foreman, but he didn't stay long before going on to the Brown Ranch where he spent the night.

Early the next morning, February 5th, Bower rode the ten miles upriver to the Boars Nest and on as far as the Vineyard Ranch to spend the night. He was able to contact the individuals at each of the ranches who needed to be in Elko for the trial on the 12th of February. Bower said he expected to run into trouble at any time and was fearful sheepmen might catch up to him and do him harm. The morning of the 6th he rode to the H.D. Ranch where he ran into Jack Davis and Fred Gleason. The three of them had dinner and together rode the rest of the way to Wells.

From Wells, Bower took the train to Reno to load the cattle, and then took the train back to Ogden, Utah. He arrived in Ogden early on the morning of the 8th of February and went directly to John Spark's hotel to report to him. He also had time to accomplish the adoption process of his step-daughter, Eva, who was to be married on February 12th.

The Board of Pardons II (1899)

The aftermath of the October board meeting left the board, composed of Gov. Frank Steunenberg, Secretary of State George Lewis and Attorney General Robert McFarland, with a dilemma. Should they believe the jury's decision that Davis was guilty as charged, a decision based largely on circumstantial evidence, or should they believe the confessions of two men who had perjured themselves in the earlier trial of Diamondfield Jack Davis?

At the December hearing the board's attention was diverted from the Diamondfield Jack issue to the newly obtained handwritten confessions of James Bower and Jeff Gray. Their attention turned more to the truthfulness and the feasibility of this new development in what was already a complex situation.

Hawley brought Bower, Gray, and a number of other witnesses to testify in person at this board meeting. A key part of Hawley's plan was for the board to hear the testimony from Bower and Gray as well as a number of other witnesses, testifying to the fact that Gray and Bower had confided in them soon after the incident about their part in the killings. The board and William Borah, the prosecuting attorney in the original Davis trial, interviewed Bower and Gray in an insinuating and almost caustic tone. Borah did not believe Bower or Gray when they claimed to have been at the scene rather than Davis.

Borah questioned Jeff Gray about testimony he had given during the Davis trial concerning his whereabouts on the morning of February 4th. Gray had testified that he did not see Bower after they parted at Goat Springs, but he now stated that he and Bower went to the sheep camp together.

Borah: "You did know that you saw him again?"

Gray: "Yes, I saw him."

Borah: “When you were testifying in the Jack Davis case did you intend to state falsely as to your whereabouts that day?”

Gray: “No, sir, I did not; I calculated to protect myself.”

Borah: “Did you intend upon that occasion to testify to a falsehood as to where you were upon that day?”

Gray: “No sir, not entirely; I did not propose to incriminate myself or break into jail.”

Borah continued to question Gray about the details of different events on the 4th of February, 1896. Gray either had a hard time remembering the events or he was being very careful with his answers to many of the questions he was being asked. Borah’s line of questioning was intended to catch Gray in a lie by trying to prove he was not at the scene as he had said in his confession.

It was obvious that Hawley and Puckett had prepared Gray and instructed him well for Borah’s relentless questioning. Borah was skilled in breaking a witness down and leading the witness to stumble into an admission of deceiving. Gray handled the interrogation well by answering “I do not remember,” rather than agreeing or disagreeing with Borah’s leading questions, which were designed to lead the witness into various traps.

Each of the three board members questioned Bower concerning the story contained in his confession. Their line of questioning clearly indicated they were not convinced of the truth of Bower’s confession.

Attorney General Robert McFarland was the first to question Bower. He asked Bower to state what happened and how it happened on the morning of the 4th of February. Bower repeated again how he and Gray came upon the sheep wagon with Wilson and Cummins preparing dinner and how, after they entered the wagon, an argument ensued between himself and Wilson. Bower explained how Wilson jumped on him and wrestled him to the floor of the camp wagon. Bower stated that he was wearing a fur overcoat and carrying a six shooter under his undercoat. With Wilson on top of him, Bower struggled to reach his gun under his coat. As Bower pulled the gun out, Wilson took it away from him. According to Gray, Wilson was about to shoot Bower, so Gray shot Wilson in order to save Bower's life.

Attorney General McFarland asked Bower, “What became of the revolver Wilson took from you during the scuffle? Bower replied, “I continued packing it with me until about six months ago, and lost it near about Minidoka."

Bower's answer raises the question as to what did happen to his gun: Was his gun lost or did he perhaps throw it away somewhere in the desert?

Present Day: The Gun

The gun and the bullet.(photo by author)

In the latter part of June 2011, I needed a piece of angle iron cut a few inches shorter.

The angle iron was part of a new table saw I recently had purchased. My friend, Dean Buckwitz, owns and operates a machine shop in Boise and I knew he would be able to cut it for me. I went to his shop with my grandson, Will, to talk with Dean about cutting the metal. Dean looked at what needed to be done and told me that I would need to bring the piece to his home shop where he kept the band saw that could cut the metal. That evening Will and I went to his home with the metal to be cut off.

After cutting and smoothing the edges, I told him about the story of Diamondfield Jack, about finding the location of the campsite and even finding a bullet at the site.

When I told Dean about finding the bullet he asked if I had anyone examine the bullet to determine if it had been shot from one of the guns used in the shooting, if the bullet was of the period, and if it was of the same caliber gun used at the time. I explained that it had been examined by at least four experts and they all agreed that it is definitely a solid lead bullet of the type used before 1900. So there is a strong possibility that it's one of the bullets fired during the incident.

Dean asked if the bullet had been tested to determine if it had been fired from one of the guns used during the shooting.

I replied that the whereabouts of those guns is not known.

He asked what happened to those guns.

I told him I had no knowledge of the location of any of them, with the exception of the gun of James Bower. I knew he had testified before the Board of Pardons in December of 1898 that he had lost his gun six months before he had come there to testify.

Dean asked what kind of gun it had been and I could only tell him that it had been a .44 caliber. I could also tell him that Bower had carried his gun under his coat in a shoulder holster. Bower described his struggle with Wilson on the floor of the wagon in his 21-page handwritten confession to the Board of Pardons, dated October 13, 1898: "I recollect having my pistol inside my under coat and as two buttons had been torn off my over coat. I reach for my pistol, and got hold of it. The man on me grasped it also, and said something about fixing me and had the pistol about away from me, when I heard a shot, which seemed to have been fired close to my head."

Dean asked me again what happened to Bower's gun and I told him again that Bower had testified that he lost it.

Dean looked at me with a quizzical look and said, "Max, I think I have that gun!"

I looked at him and asked, "What would make you think that you have that gun?"

He said, "It is not a very likely story to say he had lost the gun. It's more likely that he threw the gun away rather than losing it where it had been used in the commission of a crime."

Dean said that about four years ago his landlord came to him with a badly rusted gun and told him that his family did not know what to do with the gun, which had belonged to his recently-deceased brother. Since the brother had never married, there were no children or other family members to inherit it, and the landlord said that since Dean collected guns, he thought it should be given to him. The gun was very badly rusted, having lain in the dirt or in water for many years before the landlord's brother found it out in the desert. Even in its badly-rusted state, however, it was easily recognizable as a Colt six-gun. The grips were made of a hard rubber (Bakelite) and were well preserved with the Colt insignia clearly embossed on the handles.

Dean remembered from that conversation that the brother had spent many days treasure hunting or scouring the desert south of Mountain Home and in the Idaho mountains, looking for arrow heads and anything else he might run into. Dean remembered specifically being told that the construction company his landlord's father owned did a lot of construction down in the Rogerson and Three Creek area of southern Idaho. They also mentioned working on ranches in northern Nevada just south of the Idaho border. The landlord's brother as well as other family members would spend their free time searching in the desert looking for artifacts of the past.

An old gun lying in the desert, found by an individual searching for artifacts decades later, had to have a history behind it that would stir the imagination of history buffs. I couldn't wait to go back to Dean's shop the next day to look at the gun.

The gun was a revolver with a shorter barrel which would have been the type used with an under-the-shoulder holster. Dean made the comment about the chances of this type of gun, first, being sold in southern Idaho, second, being lost or thrown away in the vicinity of this incident. Dean emphasized the thrown away part, adding that he strongly believed the gun had been thrown away rather than lost. He pointed out that if the gun had been lost it most likely would still contain bullets. If the gun had been thrown away, the bullets would have been removed to be used in another gun. The rusty gun did not have any bullets in it. The logic made sense.

I knew John Taffin, a nationally recognized gun expert, and thought he would be someone to look at the gun. I knew he would have knowledge about guns of this type, so I took the gun to him to examine.

He had the information at his fingertips. He first brought out another gun of the same model to compare the two. Both guns were . 44-40 with a 4¾ inch barrel. John also had the manufacturer's data on that make and model. It was a model 1878 Colt Frontiersman. John said there were only 18,000 .44-40 caliber revolvers manufactured between 1880 and 1905. Of that number only 2,989 had the 4¾ inch barrel. Of the 2,989 4¾ inch-barrel revolvers manufactured, 850 of them were known to have been sent to Russia. The short barrel would have likely been used with an under-shoulder holster. With only 2,139 left in the U.S., and with two of them on the table in front of us, the odds seemed pretty high that the gun found in the desert could have been James E. Bower's gun, thrown away following the incident on Deep Creek back in 1896.

Board of Pardons III (1898)

John Sparks, Bower's boss, said in a sworn statement before the Board of Pardons on November 19, 1902 that he was awakened in his hotel room at 6:00 a.m. by James Bower on the morning of of February 8, 1896.

Sparks said Bower appeared to be greatly worried and somewhat excited. Bower told Sparks that he was in serious trouble and then proceeded to tell him about the events of the past week, including the details about coming onto the sheep camp and confronting the sheepherders, Wilson and Cummins.

After going over the facts together, Sparks and Bower tried to decide what course of action Bower needed to take at that point. Bower asked Sparks what he thought about just leaving the country, but they quickly agreed that was the wrong thing to do. Bower would have to face the charges, which would be determined by whether or not the more badly injured sheepherder survived or died.

Sparks considered Bower's statement to him as being made in confidence, so he spoke to no one about it, with the exception of A.J. Harrell, his partner. Still, he was greatly concerned about his duty in the matter. Sparks and Harrell concluded the proper course to follow was to keep silent as to their knowledge of the affair. They agreed, however, that if they were questioned by the authorities about the matter, they would fully disclose what they knew. Their silence, in other words, was not an attempt to conceal from the proper authorities or to protect anyone who had committed a crime.

Sparks stated to the Board of Pardons, "When Gleason and Davis were arrested in 1897 and charged with the murder of Wilson and Cummins, my proper course in the matter became a matter of still graver doubt with me." Both Davis and Gleason had worked for his company and Sparks knew both were innocent, but he could not make his knowledge public without violating the confidence placed in him by Bower. Neither Bower nor Gray seemed willing to make public their connection with the affair.

Sparks said he did not believe it possible to convict an innocent man, and he was unwilling to betray the confidence of a friend unless it became his duty to impart his knowledge of the matter. He discussed the matter with Bower who assured Sparks that, in the event of a conviction of either Davis or Gleason, he would make the whole matter public and would never see an innocent man punished. Sparks and Harrell both concluded the proper course for them was to defend Davis and Gleason, and if they were convicted, rely on Bower to come forth with his confession. Neither Sparks nor Harrell were called to testify in the trial of Davis and neither appeared before any court or hearing until after Bower and Gray had confessed to their part in the shooting.

When the vote was taken by the board on whether to pardon Davis it was clear one member did not believe Bower's or Gray's story, and the other two members seemed to believe enough of their story that even though they didn't grant Davis a pardon, they did give Davis yet another reprieve. This time the date of hanging was moved from December 16, 1898 to February 1, 1899, which would give them time for one more hearing to be held in January.

For the third time, the town of Albion had to anticipate and prepare yet again for a hanging that would more than likely not happen.

Attorney General McFarland wrote his dissenting opinion on the 6th day of December outlining the reasons for his dissent. He made five points in his opinion, of which four were most interesting.

- "One: The case has already been postponed twice and no good or sufficient reason exists for a continuance.
- Two: The Board, during its investigation and deliberations of petitioner's application, has had before it a transcript of all the evidence and proceedings upon which the conviction was had, and upon which the Supreme Court passed in affirming the judgment, besides the oral testimony of numerous witnesses, affidavits and counter affidavits filed by the respective parties to the proceedings, which certainly ought to be sufficient to justify decision one way or another.
- Three: The expense of the trial, and the cost and expense of maintaining and keeping the prisoner throughout the trial and proceedings in this case which have covered more than two years, have been sufficiently onerous upon Cassia County, I do

not feel disposed to inflict any further burden upon it in this behalf.

- Four: I do not believe it right or just for the retiring members of this Board to avoid the responsibility of an unpleasant duty by bequeathing it to successors."

There didn't seem to be any doubt in McFarland's mind about the guilt of Davis and the distrust of Bower and Gray.

There were also changes on the Board of Pardons.

The fall election of 1898 replaced two members of the Board of Pardons, which was then made up of elected officials. M.A. Petrie replaced George Lewis as Secretary of State, and S.H. Hays replaced Robert McFarland as Attorney General. The two new members took their place on the board in early January.

Shortly after the new board was sworn into office Jack Davis sent word that he wanted to appear personally before them and make a statement. On January 14, 1899 the *Capital News* reported:

Diamondfield Wants to Talk

Diamondfield Jack has sent word to the State Board of Pardons that he wants to say something to the Board in person and requested an opportunity to be heard. The Board has decided to give him a chance, but does not feel inclined to trust Jack out of jail, and all the members will go to Albion tomorrow to give him a hearing. They will return Tuesday. It is just possible that Diamondfield may make some sensational disclosures on this occasion."

The new board scheduled the meeting to take place in Albion on Monday, January 16, 1899. Governor Frank Steunenberg opened the hearing by asking two attorneys, Will Puckett for the defense, and William Borah, the prosecuting attorney, how the proceedings should be conducted. The agreement was to let Davis make his statement, as he had requested, and allow the board and counsel to ask questions.

Davis's first statement was, "Let Mr. Borah examine me and cross-examine me all he wants; I am perfectly willing for that."

However, as the hearing progressed Davis did not fare well under Borah's questioning.

The courtroom was filled to capacity with local citizens as well as the press anticipating perhaps a big break in the case. Instead they listened for three hours to Davis declaring his innocence and explaining all the accusations made against him by the sheepherders. He explained away every testimony against him as falsehood, stating that the witnesses perjured themselves. Much of his exhortation was rambling and incoherent.

As soon as Borah began his questions, Davis became defensive and impulsive in his responses. His sentences would break off and become disconnected. He countered with questions of his own directed to Borah and statements implicating that Borah had bought and perjured witnesses. Davis angrily said, "Mr. Borah, you know in your heart just as well as I do that I am innocent of this. You are not prosecuting, you are persecuting a man, and at the same time you are procuring witnesses and trying to make a name for yourself, and you walk over my grave to do it."

Puckett did not take the opportunity to follow up with any comments or questions to his client. He may not have wanted to give his client any additional opportunities to further hurt his case, which he was sure he had done. The assembled crowd that had thought maybe they would hear something new and possibly sensational all left disappointed.

After the three hours of testimony, the board returned to Boise to resume their deliberations on granting Jack a pardon. Besides presenting additional affidavits, a number of citizens from the Rock Creek area testified concerning conversations they had with Jeff Gray shortly after the shootings back around February 5 and 6, 1896. Hawley went to a great deal of effort to substantiate the citizenry, credibility, and veracity of J.B. Rice, Jeff Gray, James Bower, and the two Jones brothers. The main stage was taken by John Sparks, owner of the Sparks-Harrell Cattle Company and former employer of Davis, Gleason, Bower, and Gray. Sparks testified that Bower met him in Ogden, Utah around February 8 or 9, just four or five days after the shooting had taken place. He said that Bower confided in him about his participation with Jeff Gray in the shooting and explained the circumstances and how Gray did the shooting to protect Bower's life.

The sworn affidavits of Bower and Gray which stated they were responsible for the killings and not Diamondfield Jack should have had an impact on the board's deliberations. But neither those affidavits nor the sworn testimonies from some of the leading citizens of the community persuaded the board. Despite all of the affidavits and testimonies the board decided the matter didn't even warrant further investigation or questions. It appears they were of the opinion that some conspiracy was in play to protect and free Diamondfield Jack.

Apparently the interview the board had with Davis did not change any of its members' minds. They voted on January 23, 1899 to deny a pardon for Davis. Their decision read:

"We the under signed, do hereby certify that the following is a full, true and complete transcript of a RESOLUTION passed by the Board of Pardons, January 23, 1899, in the matter of the application of Jack Davis for pardon. RESOLVED: The application for pardon is denied. The Board being satisfied that the showing made does not justify interference with the verdict of the jury and the sentence of the Court."

The decision meant the February 1st hanging date remained in force and the town of Albion would have to start making the necessary preparations. As reported in the January 26, 1899, *Idaho Daily Statesman*, the news concerning the Board of Pardons' decision reached Albion on the 24th, but Sheriff Burke didn't received the registered letter until 2:30 pm on the 25th which was the official notification.

The *Idaho Statesman's* correspondent accompanied Sheriff Burke and others to the jail to convey the news to Davis. The correspondent reported:

On entering the quarter where Davis was, Jack shook hands with each of them after which the Sheriff said: "Well Jack you have got the worst of it," at the same time taking from his pocket the document from the Board of Pardons that meant so much to Davis. Jack simply replied, "All right." Sheriff Burke started to read the letter but Jack took it in his own hands read it through himself, after reading it, he handed it back to the Sheriff without saying a word. During the reading of the decision Jack seemed to be the most cool and collected man present and in conversation looked each speaker straight in the eye. On being asked whether he had anything to say Davis stated that he had nothing to say any more than that he was innocent of the crime he is charged with committing.

In way of making the necessary preparation Sheriff Burke had so far wired the Sheriff of Bingham County requesting the use of the scaffold used there some time ago. It is believed that it is now on the way.

Sheriff Burke immediately upon receipt of the official notice from the Pardon Board placed several extra guards on duty and is taking every step necessary to carry out the arrangements in compliance with law although the time is very short, the day of execution being set to Wednesday February 1, 1899 unless something intervenes to have it again postponed.

Hawley did not wait long before filing yet another appeal to stay the execution of his client. On January 28 he submitted an application to the United States District Court, Judge J.H. Beatty, for Writ of Habeas Corpus. The *Capital News* reported Hawley's actions:

"Diamondfield Jack" will not hang on the first of February. For at least 30 days he will pace his gloomy cell and at times look out upon the sun shining in the heavens and breathe the delightful air. But he still stands face to face with death, linked to the veritable body of the grim conqueror by chains so strong, so adamantine that it is a question whether the court of last resort will break them.

This morning Hon. James Hawley filed in Federal District Court, Judge J. H. Beatty, a petition for a writ of habeas corpus in the case of "Diamondfield Jack" now in the very shadow of the gallows. The petition asserts that the said Jack Davis is wrongfully and unlawfully detained in the county jail of Cassia County, Idaho, by virtue of certain proceedings, judgments and orders.

Judge Beatty reviewed the application and listened to the argument by Hawley but very shortly afterward denied the petition for a Writ of Habeas Corpus. An appeal from his decision was taken to the Circuit Court of Appeals in San Francisco. That appeal automatically gave Davis a new lease on life, since under the federal statutes a man is entitled to an appeal in such case and is also entitled to a stay of proceedings. There is no discretion left with the court.

After considering the matter and conferring with Idaho's Attorney General Hays, Judge Beatty made the peremptory order to stay the proceedings until the appeal could have a hearing in the Circuit Court of Appeals in San Francisco.

With the execution scheduled to happen the next morning, February 1, W.H. Puckett left the afternoon of January 31 on the train for the 175-mile trip to Albion in order to personally deliver Judge Beatty's order to Sheriff Burke. Hawley also wired a notice of the issuance of the order to be delivered from Minidoka to Albion to alert the sheriff just in case something might delay Puckett's delivery.

Puckett arrived early the morning of February 1. Despite Sheriff Burke's preparation, the city was deprived of the hanging of "Diamondfield Jack" for the fourth time. The appeal to the Circuit Court of Appeals would give Davis another extended period of jail time.

In the Penitentiary (1899)

Due to legislation passed by the 1899 legislature, however, Davis would not be waiting out the appeal process sitting in his cell in Albion. On February 16th the legislature passed a law which relieved sheriffs from the unpleasant duty of carrying out executions in their counties. The state penitentiary would, in the future, witness all executions of criminals in the state. The *CAPITAL NEWS* reported the passage of the law with this headline:

NECKTIE PARTIES AT THE PEN, All Future Execution Will Take Place at that Institution. As the measure carries an emergency clause it will cover the execution of "Diamondfield Jack," providing he is ever hung.

Shortly thereafter 'Diamondfield Jack' was transported to the State Penitentiary in Boise to fret his fate.

The *Statesman* reported Davis's trip to Boise on Monday morning February 28, 1899:

He was brought in on the train from the east last night by special guards Hugh Fulton, and Sam Howdy, appointed to go after him. Davis showed himself to be a man of iron nerve and at times during the trip his eyes would flash with the terrible light that has so often been noted by those who have known him. He is a small man and looked like a pigmy between his stalwart guards.

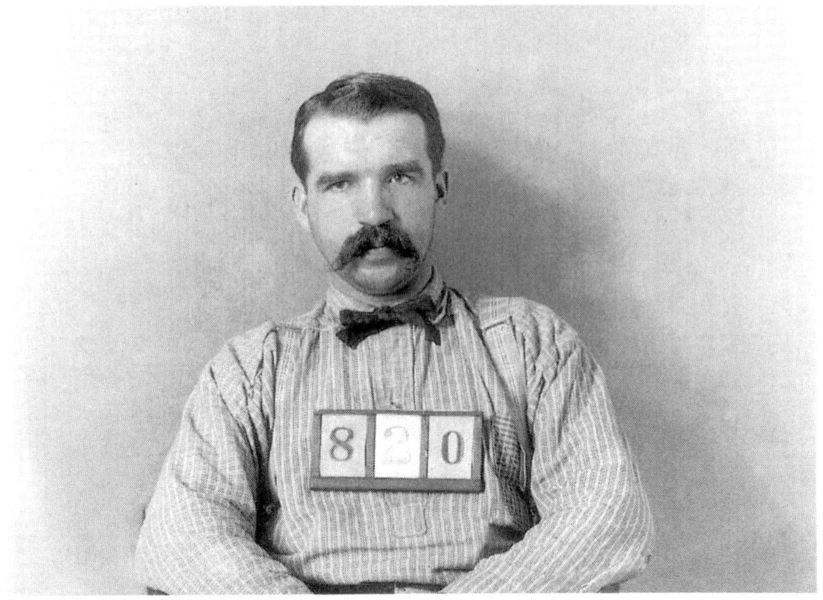

Jackson Lee Davis being admitted into the State Penitentiary. (photo courtesy Idaho Historical Society)

The Statesman never supported Hawley through the entire case and their description of Davis in this instance was a little ill-flavored. Davis would wait out his appeal in Boise for the time being while justice took its course.

During the month of February there were a lot of conversations in Boise as well southern Idaho about the Diamondfield Jack case. Back in Albion a new legal battle was taking place over the arrest and pending trial of Jeff Gray and James E. Bower and at the same time the legislature set off the dispute as to where Jack Davis was to be executed. Back in November 1898 James E. Bower and Jeff Gray had confessed to the killing and were charged with their deaths. Gray's trial was scheduled for the February term in Albion, and Bower's was to take place shortly after Gray's.

Gray and Bower at trial (1899)

As the time for Gray's trial neared and the prosecution and defense organized their legal arguments, Borah also had to position himself to protect the guilty verdict he had obtained on Jack Davis.

William. E. Borah appeared before Judge Stockslager and argued for a motion for a continuance of the case against J. E. Bower for participation in the murder of Cummings and Wilson. Borah argued that if Bower had any part in the killing it was as an accomplice of Davis and it would take time to gather the evidence to support that charge.

The judge agreed and the motion for a continuance was granted. This meant that Bower would not have a trial until a later time.

Cassia County's new prosecuting attorney, B.P. Howells, inherited the job of prosecuting Bower and Gray from John Rogers, the retiring prosecuting attorney for the county who had worked with Borah in convicting Diamondfield Jack. Rogers held a preliminary hearing for Jeff Gray and felt there was sufficient evidence to charge him with the murder of John Wilson and Daniel Cummins.

Howells was reluctant to take Gray to trial with the only real evidence to convict being his confession and that of Bower. Their confessions stated that they had gone to the victim's camp, gotten into a fight and shot Wilson and Cummings in self-defense. Twice Howells sent over documents to Judge Stockslager that stated:

"...that after thoroughly investigating the case and having looked into the evidence which can be had that there is no possible chance to secure a conviction in the case. I further state that with the evidence now to be had that I am convinced as public prosecutor that there is no foundation for the charge made that the said Jeff D. Gray had anything to do with the killing of John C. Wilson or Daniel Cummins."

Hawley strenuously objected to Howell's motion, claiming it was the right of his client to have a trial while witnesses were available. Judge Stockslager took Hawley's position and declined to dismiss the case. The Judge said, "There will be a trial at the present term."

Gray's trial commenced on February 16 with B.P. Howells as the prosecuting attorney and James Hawley, Esq., W.L. McGuinness, Esq. and J.W. Dorsey as the defense attorneys.

When the trial got underway, twenty witnesses were lined up to testify. The first three men to testify established that a crime had been committed near Deep Creek and the two victims, John C. Wilson and Daniel Cummings had been shot and both died from their wounds. The first three witnesses had been present at the site when the inquest was held by the sheriff on the 18th of February, 1896. They laid out the particulars of the investigation by Sheriff Perkins and the autopsy by Dr. Story. They also described the evidence found in and around the camp wagon. The next six witnesses all testified that Gray had confided to them soon after the shooting that he, not Davis, was the one who had shot the two victims. A total of eleven witnesses including the six that Gray had confided in, testified to the good character and good reputation of Gray as a citizen of the community.

J.E. Burke, sheriff of Cassia County, was asked during his testimony how long he had known Jeff Gray. He replied that he had known Gray since 1884.

The questioning continued:

Question: "Do you know what his general reputation was for peace and quietude in his community prior to February 4, 1896?"

Answer: "It was good!"

Question: "Do you know his general reputation for truth and veracity in the community where he lived prior to that time?"

Answer: "It was good!"

Jeff Gray continued to live and work in the same general area for a number of years following this incident. I never found any information about him that suggested he was not respected and known as a good citizen in his community.

Both Gray and Bower testified as to their part in the shootings. They gave the details of riding together that morning and coming upon the sheep camp which resulted in an argument and ultimately the shootings in self-defense. Hawley's strategy in this trial was basically the same as it had been before the Board of Pardons. Hawley had to convince the jury that Gray was telling the truth, a task which he had apparently not been able to accomplish before the Board of Pardons.

One advantage in this trial that he'd not had not at the board hearing was that the jury was made up of local citizens—Gray's neighbors and contemporaries who knew him to be a solid citizen; Gray also did not have the reputation that Davis had as a braggart and troublemaker. The following Tuesday, the 21st, after four days of testimony, the judge gave the jury his instructions and they went into deliberations. It required all of fifteen minutes for the jury to reach a verdict. They gave the judge a handwritten note with their decision on it, which read, "We the jury impounded herein find the defendant Jeff D. Gray not guilty. Signed, R. L. Ward, Foreman."

The verdict of not guilty was no help to Davis. A guilty verdict would have accomplished Hawley's purpose quickly, but "not guilty" left Davis convicted. Two days later, on the 23rd, Hawley was successful in obtaining the signatures of 11 of the 12 jurors on an affidavit stating:

"We did believe from the evidence that he was there at said killing and did kill those men, as stated in his evidence, the evidence of James Bower, and that he was acquitted, as far as our votes were concerned, upon the ground and for the reason that it was shown by said testimony that the shots fired by the said Gray were fired by him in defense of J.E. Bower and himself. Gray was justifiable in the shooting."

If Gray had been found guilty Davis would have to been released, but this would have presented a new set of problems for Gray and Bower. With the affidavit signed by the jury that Gray had shot the two men in self-defense, Hawley felt he had the evidence he needed to convince the Board of Pardons to overthrow Davis's conviction or at least grant Davis a pardon.

The new law passed by the legislature removing Davis to the state penitentiary changed the dynamics of the case. This change in law opened the case up for some possible new legal maneuvering by Hawley. Borah, anticipating that Hawley might try a new legal maneuver, took the offensive to thwart a possible unintended consequence of Davis being caught in between two laws. Sometime after Davis was transferred from Albion to the penitentiary in Boise, Sheriff Burke of Cassia County, and Borah, sued in the Idaho Supreme Court for a *habeas corpus* writ to regain custody of Davis.

The passage of the new law would in effect repeal the old law under which Davis was convicted and make him subject to the new law. This raised a number of questions. First, was the new law unconstitutional and void by reason of it being *ex post facto*? Second, if so, was the old law repealed by virtue of the new law—or, in other words, under which law must the sentence resting upon Davis be carried out? A further question presented itself: "Did the amendment of said Section 8021 repeal its provisions as to the execution of the death sentence as they existed prior to the amendment, and thus leave no law under which said sentence may be executed and because thereof permit Davis to escape the judgment pronounced against him? In other words, *would* "Diamondfield" be pardoned by legislation?"[14]

Hawley and Puckett appeared before the court, *amicus curiae,* (friends of the court) and argued the finer points of the law before the bench, pointing out how the U.S. Supreme Court had ruled in previous cases in other states with similar laws. The court had ruled that such laws were *ex post facto* and did in fact repeal the old law, which would leave no law by which the judgment against Davis could be executed.

Borah and Idaho Attorney General S.H. Hays argued for the petitioner, Sheriff Burke, contending that Idaho had a statute which served as a general saving clause for all criminal statutes which prevented the repeal of an old criminal law. That statute reads:

"Sec 59. The repeal of any law creating a criminal offense does not constitute a bar to the indictment and punishment of an act already committed in violation of the law so repealed, unless the intention to bar such indictment and punishment is expressly declared in the repealing act."[15]

Davis now had to sit in his cell in the penitentiary at Boise from February 28, 1899, waiting for the decision from both the Idaho Supreme Court and the Federal Court of Appeals in San Francisco, to which Hawley had appealed a month earlier.

Decisions in both appeals were not made until the fall of 1899. On October 21 the Circuit Court of Appeals dismissed the appeal from

14 From Idaho Supreme Court, December 22, 1899.

15 Idaho Supreme Court Decision *State vs Jack Davis*, Dec, 22,1899.

Federal Judge Beatty's District Court. The Circuit Court denied the appeal and based their decision on the lack of jurisdiction. Hawley had successfully kept Davis in his cell rather than the execution block.

On December 23, 1899, the Idaho Supreme Court ruled on Sheriff Burke's *habeas corpus* case against John Hailey, warden of the state penitentiary.

On the question of whether the new law repealed the provisions as to the execution of the death sentence as they existed prior to the new law, leaving no law under which the sentence could be executed and thus permitting Davis to escape the judgment pronounced against him, the court ruled in favor of the petitioner, the sheriff of Cassia County, giving him custody of Davis. The court wrote: "It is therefore ordered that Jack Davis be committed to the custody of the petitioner, *J.E. Burke, Sheriff of Cassia County, to be dealt with according to law and the authority of the court having jurisdiction in the premises.*"[16]

This ruling gave Davis yet another train ride, this one back to his cell in Albion. Davis sat safely in his cell in Albion, protected by the stay of execution issued by the Circuit Court of Appeals in February 1899. Following the ruling of the Circuit Court in October, no court had reset an execution date for Davis.

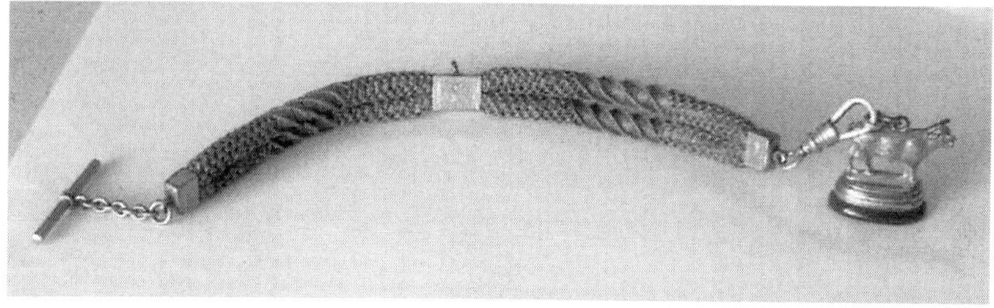

Watch fob made by Jack from the hair of Alice Terrill. Owned by Betty Waggner, daughter of Alice Terrill. (photo by author)

During the summer and fall of 1899 both Borah and Hawley were busy working the trials surrounding the violence at the mines in Northern Idaho. The publicity generated by those trials overshadowed "Diamondfield" during this period, so Jack spent most of his time

16 Idaho Supreme Court Decision *State vs Jack Davis*, Dec, 22,1899.

making small souvenirs which he often gave away to people who had befriended him.

In the latter part of March 1900, Hawley again made application to the 9th Circuit Court for writ of *habeas corpus* on behalf of his client. The 9th Circuit Court heard the appeal but required only a few days to hear the case and refuse the petition.

This refusal opened the way for the petition to be appealed to the U.S. Supreme Court. The 9th Circuit Court, at the same time, put another stay on all proceedings until the U.S. Supreme Court could hear the case in their fall term, which meant at least another nine months of waiting for Davis. The U.S. Supreme Court made their decision on December 23, 1900. This was the second Supreme Court decision which came almost on Christmas Eve for Davis. Waiting in his cell of course was preferable to experiencing an execution, but as time moved on it seemed to take longer and longer between appeals being made and action being taken by the courts. Davis had been waiting from February 1899 under a stay of proceedings until April of 1900, and again on April 2, 1900 the 9th Circuit Court issued another stay which remained in force until the following April, 1901.

With the highest court in the land turning down his appeal in December 1900, it was time for Hawley to try another legal maneuver, this time back in the original court where it had all started four years earlier, the District Court of the Fourth Judicial District of Idaho in Cassia County.

The original judge, Judge Stockslager, had since moved on to the Idaho Supreme Court and the new judge was Judge George H. Stewart, who wrote, "The defendant through his Attorneys made application for a new trial based upon newly discovered evidence in regard to the killing of Wilson by Jeff D. Gray instead of the defendant. Various affidavits were filed in support of the motion, and the Court having heard the argument on 26th day of April, 1901 overruled the motion and proceeded to sentence Davis to be hanged, fixing the date for the execution of said sentence for June 21st 1901."

Hawley, his attorney, immediately appealed to the Idaho Supreme Court. The appeal to the Supreme Court did not automatically carry a stay of execution, so June 21st was fixed for the execution.

This situation left Hawley with only one option: Petition the Board of Pardons, once again, for relief. An application to that board was made requesting a hearing during their July session which if accepted would automatically include at least a temporary stay of execution.

As the June 21st deadline approached, neither the Board of Pardons nor the Supreme Court had responded with either an acceptance or denial. Finally, on the 17th of June, the Supreme Court issued a decision not to intervene, which left the June 21st execution date in place.

The sheriff was preparing to take the scaffold out of storage.

On the same day the Supreme Court issued its decision, the Board of Pardons moved the hanging date to July 3, 1901. The pardons board had set their meeting time to 10 o'clock on July 3, 1901. Special precautions were put in place in order that Sheriff Brown of Cassia County would get the word from the board. The morning of July 4,1901 the *Statesman* reported the happenings of the previous day:

"The state board met yesterday morning in the office of secretary of State Bassett. It was called to order at 10 o'clock. At 10:05 the following telegram was flashed over the wires to Minidoka.

Boise, Idaho. July 3.-M. T Brown

Albion, Idaho: In the meeting today board of pardons have extended the respite of Jack Davis from July 3 to July 17, Acknowledge receipt of this by wire and mail.

F.W. Hunt,

C.J. Bassett'

Frank Martin.

Board of Pardons.

The message then need to be relayed onto Albion, where "Diamondfield" Jack lies in jail, and where Sheriff Brown of Cassia County was in waiting to carry out the behests of the Board. Two men were in waiting at the Minidoka telegraph office, waiting to speed to the county seat at the instant a telegraph was received. Relays of horses were set up making practically certain that the 30 miles between the two places would be covered in not more than two hours.

Anticipating the decision which the Board of Pardons would make, Hawley had made the necessary arrangements to assure that Sheriff Brown would receive the information he needed to stay the execution, scheduled for Wednesday July 3, on time.

A telephone line had been put into place from Minidoka over to Albion around the turn of the century but Hawley feared that someone could foul up the line along the way. As a backup arrangement, two riders were stationed at the telegraph office in Minidoka to relay the message on to Albion as soon as it was received. Separate routes were established for the two riders, and three additional horses for each rider were stationed along the way to make sure the message would easily arrive within two hours.

The two riders were Willis Sears and Charles Krise. Both young men would long be remembered by Jack Davis for their part in the staying of his execution that day. The one rider, 20-year-old Willis Sears, was very familiar with the route to Albion. Willis' father owned a stage line between the two towns and he had driven the stage over and back many times since his teen years. Delivering the telegram on that day played a pivotal and memorable part in his life; Jack Davis and Willis Sears would become business partners five years later in Goldfield, Nevada.

During the meeting before the board on July 3, Hawley asked for a postponement until July 11 to prepare and arrange for witnesses to be present at a full hearing. At the meeting on July 11, Hawley brought all of the evidence he had accumulated over the past four years. He thought the most compelling new evidence was the affidavit signed by the eleven jurors from Jeff Gray's trial. The affidavit stated that the jury had found Jeff innocent of the first degree murder of John Wilson, but they did believe Gray shot Wilson in self-defense. Hawley had been unable to present this new evidence before any court or the Board of Pardons since Gray's trial back in February 1899. He had great hopes that this new evidence, along with the number of respected local citizens testifying to Bower's and Gray's admitting to them soon after the event about their part in the killings, would convince the board of Davis's innocence.

Hawley was also prepared with numerous letters and affidavits signed by citizens stating their conviction that Davis was unjustly convicted with circumstantial evidence heavily influenced by prejudice of the community, which was caused largely by the open conflict between the sheepmen and cattlemen. In a letter to the board, dated June 20, 1901, from Charles S. Mark, editor and publisher of the *Albion Times,* outlined the change in public opinion from the time of Davis's conviction and the current situation:

Since the confession of Bower and Gray there has been a decided change in public opinion and many who were formerly outspoken in their utterances against Davis now say they feel certain a mistake was made and that he should be released.

Hawley put a great deal of emphasis on what appeared to be a general change of opinion in the area. He introduced petitions for the pardon of Jack Davis signed by 784 persons from Albion, Oakley, Rock Creek, and Cassia County in general.

Hawley then presented several affidavits from individuals stating that Jeff Gray had told them on several occasions about having shot the two sheepherders. The first was Charles S. Hewitt, manager for the Sparks-Harrell Cattle Company. The next was R. T. Robinson, a Cassia County rancher, who alleged that a drunk Jeff Gray, during the trial of Jack Davis, shouted on the street, "By God, I killed them fellers." Robinson stated in his deposition that he tried to make Gray stop talking of the matter but succeeded only after some considerable time. Mrs. Lon V. Robinson's affidavit came next. She alleged she had several times heard Jeff Gray say he had killed Wilson and Cummings.

Henry Harris had testified before the Board of Pardon in 1898 and his testimony was read again to the board. Henry was a foreman at the Middle Stack Ranch in February 1896 and had been a witness in the Jack Davis trial in addition to his later testimony given before the board.

Harris had been with John Sparks since working for Sparks in Texas as a house servant. Harris was a black man and moved with Sparks from Texas to Reno, Nevada, where he wanted to become a cowboy and work with cattle. Sparks encouraged him Harris developed into a top cowboy. He was recognized by the other employees as a knowledgeable and skillful handler of cattle and he became a respected foreman and ranch manager of several of Spark's ranches, ultimately owning his own ranch. He was fondly and respectfully referred to by employees, neighbors—and himself—as Nigger Henry. Les Sweeney, from Payette, Idaho, recently published a book about Henry Harris' life and admittance to the Cowboys Hall of Fame.

Harris testified that Jeff Gray came to him and stated, "Fred Gleason requested I go to Albion during the Davis trial and speak with him." During the visit Henry made the statement to Jeff, "I don't think the boys killed those fellers at Deep Creek." Harris said Jeff replied, "I know they didn't, I did the killing; I had to do it to save myself and Mr. Bower." Harris said the conversation was just between the two of them and so he never repeated to anyone until Jeff Gray was being tried for the killing. His testimony was considered by everyone as truthful.

Hawley called State Treasurer J.J. Plumer, who had experimented with .44 caliber shells fired in a .45 caliber revolver. He found that invariably the shell would expand or break, and that usually the shell would expand to the size of the revolver from which it was shot. In other testimony it was pointed out that the .44 shells found at the scene all fit back into a .44 revolver, unlike .44 shells that would have expanded if fired from a .45 caliber revolver.

Hawley then presented testimony from several Cassia County residents. Alex Gray (a brother of Jeff), Henry Jones (a brother-in-law), and Albert Jones (a brother to Henry Jones) all testified that Jeff Gray had told them about his shooting two sheepherders on Deep Creek. Buck Rice made the same statement about being told of the shooting by Jeff Gray. The Attorney General asked Rice whether he investigated the shooting when he learned of it, since the site was only two or three miles from his ranch and he could have determined the condition of the two wounded or dead sheepmen. Rice replied that it did not occur to him that it was the duty of a citizen to go and see if two men were in need of assistance. A.D. Norton, a rancher in Cassia County for more than 20 years, was next to testify. *The Statesman* described Norton as "a positive, sarcastic gentleman, whose answers were secured a good deal like a dentist draws refractory teeth."

The Statesman further reported:

Mr. Martin, the Attorney General, crossed-examined the gentleman closely. He would not give a direct answer to a single direct question, his animus against the sheepmen being very apparent and most bitter. He said everyone was afraid of the sheepmen and that he had considered they had no occasion to make ado about the shooting of these two or one. As he sat in the chair and recalled the flourishing of the gun and the appearance of a herder's outfit, he shook with anger, or something very akin.

Two of the most notable individuals to appeal to the board were two judges, one a current judge and the other an ex-supreme court justice from Utah. At the time of Davis' original trial they were part of the prosecuting team, along with William Borah.. Judge O.W. Powers sent two letters to the board, one dated June 16, 1901 and again on June 24, 1901 stating his change of position on the guilt of Davis. Judge Powers stated he had carefully studied the manuscripts of the testimonies taken in the case of Jeff Gray and compared it with the testimonies of the State vs. Jack Davis and as a result changed his mind about Davis' guilt and was satisfied that that the sentence of Jack Davis, alias Diamondfield Jack, should be commuted. He pointed out that he had been employed by the wool growers of Cassia County to assist the prosecution in the Jack Davis trial as well as the case against Fred Gleason—both involving the same crime and facts, and in the last named case the defendant was found not guilty by a verdict of the jury.

He further represented that he assisted in the argument of the Davis case before the Supreme Court of the State of Idaho, but since at that time he had no connection with litigation and at the present time he had no professional relation to the matter and was not in the employ of any party or person connected in any way in the matter, he made the statement solely from a sense of duty.

Judge Powers stated, "...he believes and respectfully asks in the name of justice, that the sentence of Jack Davis be commuted. Deponent feels that there is too much question about his guilt to allow the death penalty to be imposed. The evidence was circumstantial and circumstantial evidence often points in the wrong direction. The man Gleason was acquitted and if Davis is guilty Gleason is guilty. Two other men have sworn that they are the guilty parties. It is appalling for the law to take the life of a human creature when so much doubt arises as his guilt as in the present State."[17]

The second was Judge J.C. Rogers the Cassia County Prosecuting Attorney at the time of Davis's trial. Judge Rogers, like Powers, testified he had had a change of mind as to Davis's guilt. Both stated

---

17 Sworn Testimony of O. W. Powers submitted to the Board of Pardon June 24,1901.

they had served on the prosecution team and firmly believed at the time that Davis was guilty, but had since changed their minds and now felt strongly that the new evidence cleared him.

Judge Rogers stated the reason for his change of mind was his study of the testimony of hitherto honorable men, saying, "I cannot believe a whole neighborhood will deliberately lie." Roger's most compelling statement was made in his letter to the board in which he wrote, "In conclusion I am constrained to say that my conviction has grown with my investigation, and that the case of State against Jack Davis will have to go down with a long line of similar cases found in the books where strong combinations of circumstances has led an honest jury to a false conclusion—the conviction of a man innocent of the crime charged against him." Rogers also stated that a brother of J.W. Walker, the man who met and talked to Gleason at the Brown Ranch on February 3rd, said he had seen Bower on the range on the 4th and he felt sure it was Bower in the creek washing his hands.[18]

Hawley presented several letters to the board from prominent citizens in Cassia County, stating their feelings concerning the conviction of Davis and their wishes for a pardon. Hawley stated that he had in his possession letters from 50 men of the county expressing their belief in Davis's innocence. Some citizens felt the conviction was a result of prejudice and the emotional reaction of the community when two of their own were killed in what was perceived as a cold-blooded murder. W.D. Fuller from Albion wrote in his letter that shortly after Davis's trial the foreman of the jury and two others of the jury told him that, " If Davis wasn't guilty he had done enough and ought to hang on general principles." Fuller further stated in his letter the County Attorney's wife (Mrs. Howells) said in his house that "they wouldn't prosecute Bower and Gray for the killing because if they did Davis would get away from them." H.R. Cahoon, the foreman on Davis's trial, wrote a letter to the Board of Pardons and reaffirmed that he still felt strongly about Davis's guilt. Frank Bedke from Basin, two miles east of Oakley, wrote, "When Davis had his trial the County was in an uproar. The people where prejudiced against Davis, under the excitement." Hardy Sears, a county commissioner at the time of the Davis trial, said he "could now plainly see the actions of the people at the time were due to prejudice against Davis." He said, "Everyone knew or thought they knew he was guilty but now public opinion has

18 Letter from Rogers to the Board, July 8, 1901.

greatly changed since that time." S.P. Weatherman, Probate Judge of Cassia County, wrote that he "felt strongly that Davis was wrongfully convicted and if executed will be equivalent to almost, if not, murder." O.P. Anderson, Sheriff of Cassia County, had written to the board in October 1898, stating he, "...did not believe that Davis was guilty primarily due to the impossibility of a man or horse being able to go the distance from the Brown ranch up to the site of the killing and then down to the Boars Nest in the time reported." O.R. Hale, attorney-at-law, wrote in his letter, "I deem it my duty to say that the hanging of Jack Davis would be a judicial murder in my judgment."

Hawley concluded his presentation to the board by presenting a long list of leading Cassia County citizens in favor of a pardon, including the current Sheriff, M.T. Brown, who said he was confident Davis was innocent.

This concluded the testimony for the defense. District Attorney B.P Howells then said he had but one witness to put on the stand: William E. Borah.

Borah testified that he remained convinced Davis was the guilty one but was also convinced Bower was somehow equally involved. The three attorneys who served on the prosecution worked on this theory for some time but were unable to discover any substantial evidence to support it. He challenged both Judge Rogers and Judge Powers over their change of mind. Borah stated that at the time of Davis's trial the evidence had been sufficient to convince three attorneys, a judge, and the twelve jurors, and had since been before the Idaho Supreme Court, two federal circuit courts, and the United States Supreme Court, and the conviction had not been overturned. Borah remained convinced of Davis's guilt.

Hawley started his final argument before the board on Monday afternoon, July 15. He spoke for two and a half hours.

The next morning the *Capital News* reported his closing argument in part:

The Attorney made as eloquent a plea as was ever heard in Idaho, and whatever the outcome it was understood that all the argument and pleading possible was presented by the Attorney in summing up the case; to save the life of a man of whose guilt there is not only a serious question, but ample proof to substantiate his complete innocence, as Mr. Hawley expressed it. He spoke of the efforts of a Boise newspaper which for four years, he said had been directed to warping the statements of witnesses and others connected with the case in an effort to mold sentiment against Davis. He said, "...there is an innocent man standing in the shadow of the gallows, that if there is a scintilla of evidence that there has been an error made and Davis is perhaps not the guilty person, this would be sufficient to detain his execution; but in light of the abundance of new testimony, all of which proves that the killing was done by another, there can be but one verdict—and that is for you to restore to Jack Davis the liberty he enjoyed previous to March 1897."

District Attorney Howells then made his argument against the granting of a pardon. He spoke for an hour and, according to the *Statesman*, his speech was an able one.

He said they "had listened to the eloquent argument of the defense, and now as prosecuting attorney for Cassia County, I will try and enlighten the Board as to the true status of the case." He went on to say, "There was nothing new brought before this Pardon Board but what was considered by the board at two former sessions, except the theories of Judge Rodgers. Mr. Borah had gone over these and holds the same opinion as he did at the trial."

In conclusion, Howells asked on behalf of his constituents in Cassia County that the Board take no action in the matter other than to deny the pardon of Davis.[19]

At 4:30 p.m. on July 15, 1901, the Pardon Board commuted the death sentence of Jack Davis to life imprisonment.

This reprieve came the night before Davis's seventh sentence to die by hanging was to be carried out.

Each hanging date was followed by a timely reprieve by a court or the governor of the state. One would wonder how these hanging dates, and then in some cases reprieves, some of them received just hours

19 *Idaho Statesman*, July 15,1901.

before the scheduled hanging, may have worked on Davis's mind. The same could be said about the sheriffs and their staffs making preparations for the event.

The Statesman had a far different view on the proceedings. Their editorial byline read on July 15, 1901:

"DECEPTION"

The Statement made by Mr. Hawley when on the witness stand before the board of pardons was very interesting when viewed in the light of the deception surrounding the entire case of Jack Davis. Mr. Hawley implied that he had himself been deceived, in a sense of those appearing in the interest of the defense. That must have been true, for he put witnesses on the stand who testified falsely, as they have since alleged. It follows that those men, particularly Gray and Bower, did not tell him the truth.

It was deception at the beginning and it is deception at the end. Those responsible for it do not care how badly they may deceive counsel; it is Justice that they seek to deceive ultimately, and they will stop at nothing to accomplish that purpose. See the tools that are brought here in the interest of this conspiracy

It has been deception, deception, deception, and perjury to bolster up deception!

The *Evening Capital News* ran an editorial the evening of July 15 just hours after the board had made their decision to commute Davis' sentence to life imprisonment. *The Capital News* had a different view of Hawley's efforts to save Davis's life, as well as his innocence of the crime for which he had been convicted. In response to the *Idaho Statesman*'s editorial *The Capital News* byline read:

"WHO HAS BEEN DECEIVED"

In an editorial in this morning's issue, the Statesman argues that Mr. Hawley, senior counsel for Jack Davis, had been deceived by interested parties, and as a result of that deception was urging for the release of a guilty man. The reason the Statesman gives for that conclusion are as groundless as the other assertions heretofore made by this organ in regards to this affair. The article in question states that Mr. Hawley's intimation of the part played by Bower and Gray in the Deep Creek tragedy came to him through an anonymous letter. Such is not the evidence. Mr. Hawley in his evidence states that he had grave suspicions shortly after the trial in regard to Bower and Gray; that his investigations both before and after the supreme court had taken action caused him to be satisfied that the men charged were not guilty; and that circumstances which had seemingly been concealed from the defense by the prosecution , and of which the prosecution had knowledge at the time of the trial, but of which he was not then informed, caused him to suspicion strongly that Bower and Gray were the guilty men. That his investigation in Idaho and Nevada in the summer 1898 strongly confirmed his belief, and that his then colleague in the case, Judge Perky, informed him in regard to circumstances coming under his observation, and which tended more strongly to confirm the opinion. That after reaching Boise City after an extended trip over the range, during which he obtained much valuable information, tending to fasten the crime where it belonged, he found a letter postmarked at Butte P. O. and unsigned, which stated that Bower and Gray had killed Wilson and Cummings, and that the writer was satisfied that Buck Rice and Henry Jones had been informed in regard to the affair. It was not the letter that caused his conclusion as to the guilt of Bower and Gray, as the letter was only in line with the conclusion already reached by himself and Judge Perky by reason of their investigation.....being satisfied from his investigation that he discovered the true facts in the case, he wrote to his employer, the Sparks-Harrell Company in regard to the matter, also to the District Attorney John C. Rogers, giving his belief and the grounds of it, also to Mr. Bower, making peremptory demand upon him to come to Boise City at once, and relate the circumstances of the killing.

It was under these conditions and when the knowledge came home to the guilty parties, that the facts, if not known were upon the point of being discovered, and being aware from these letters that a vigorous prosecution would be instituted, and perhaps an awakening of conscience prompting them to do justice to an innocent man suffering from their crime, that Messrs. Bower and Gray were impelled to make the statements they did. Gray, however, it will be remembered, did not make his statement until a month after Bower had made the matter public, and only after consultation with others whom he had confidence, did he return to Idaho and deliver himself up. It would seem impossible, therefore, from these facts in the case for Mr. Hawley to have been deceived..... Without attempting to forestall the judgment of the board of pardons or impress upon that tribunal our views upon the matter, we think that in the interest of justice and fair play we are justified in saying that the evidence discloses that the prosecution and not defense has been deceived in this case.

Commuting Davis's death penalty to life imprisonment was of course good news and bad news to Hawley and Davis. His life had been spared but his freedom still was denied.

Reviewing the minutes of the Board of Pardons for the date of July 15, 1901 the decision of the board was expressed:

"The board duly considered all the evidence introduced and the facts introduced before said board. The facts and the circumstances giving rise to doubt in the minds of the members of the Board as to whether or not the applicant actually participated in the killing for which he was convicted; it was unanimously ordered by the Board that the sentence of the said Jack Davis be commuted from the sentence of death imposed by the judgment of the District Court of the Fourth Judicial District of the State of Idaho, in and for the County of Cassia, to a sentence of imprisonment in the State Penitentiary of the State of Idaho, at hard labor, for the balance of his natural life."

Members of the Board of Pardons stated that since there was a doubt in their minds as to whether the crime was committed by Davis, they could do nothing less than commute the sentence to life in prison. The ballistic test, conducted in their presences where 100 .44 cal. shells, were fired from a .45 cal. revolver and the majority of the shells swelled or ruptured and could not fit back into .45 cal. revolver was the convincing evidence that placed the doubt in their minds. Since Davis was carrying a .45 cal. revolver that day he must not have been the person that fired the shots killing the two men.

Despite the confessions of Bower and Gray, testimonies of numerous individuals to the effect they had been told of the details of the killings soon after the occurrence in February 1896, the appearance of J.C. Rogers and Orlando W. Powers must have had a big influence on the thinking of the board, but they could use the physical evidence surrounding the ballistic test as their reason for turning the case in a new direction.

Removing the death sentence was welcomed by Hawley and his client but was still puzzling in light of their statement as there being a doubt in their minds that Davis participated in the killings. Perhaps the board felt they had to be convinced beyond a reasonable doubt that Davis did not commit the killings and perhaps their decision was partiality politically motivated.

Charles S. Mark, the editor of the *Albion Times,* in a letter to the Board dated June 20, 1901 clearly explained the political and social climate in Oakley and Cassia County at the time.

... It is nothing but prejudice that is bringing him to the gallows ... "He ought to be hung on general principles," is a remark heard here every day. That is not justice ... My honest opinion about the matter is that it is nothing more than a political fight pure and simple. The republicans have brought the matter into every campaign since 1896, and not one man who ever signed a petition favorable to Jack Davis can get a vote out of Oakley...

I ask as a personal favor that you take my word for the truth of the statements I make and grant Davis at least a chance to live down the prejudice that has brought him where he is. Commute his sentence to life imprisonment and give him a chance to prove who committed the crime....

Very respectfully yours,

C. S. Mark

The two letters from Judge Powers and Judge Rogers combined with letter of Editor Charles S. Mark most likely had a large impact on the board's collective thinking and decision.

When the word was received in Albion about the board's decision to commute Davis's sentence there was a general sense of relief in the community. The July 18, 1901 *Statesman* recorded the historic day with a touch of sarcasm:

"ALBION SOCIAL EVENT"

The state penitentiary guards arrived in Albion at 3:00 o'clock Tuesday afternoon to escort Davis back to Boise later that night by buggy and train. The news spread quickly that they were there, and that Davis would be taken away during the night. From that time till dark there was a perfect stream of visitors to the Murderer's quarters.

Fathers and Mothers went to see him, bearings tokens of regard and of remembrance and with them they took their little children. It is said that fully two-thirds of the people of the place visited the jail before admission was denied. A morbid curiosity seemed to actuate the large number of these, and knowing Davis's penchant for flowers, nearly all brought bouquets.

Some presents of intrinsic value were made to him. Deputy Sheriff Adams gave him a gold filled, open faced watch with handsome chain; others brought books, magazines and little trinkets, which they told Jack he must keep to "remember" them by. He said he would. Later in the night he worked on a box in which to put his treasures. The box was brought to Boise and now peacefully reposes in the warden's office at the penitentiary.

Sheriff Brown treated Davis to an elegant spread for dinner that evening. "Everything that market affords" was on the table. Jack liked every bite he took. He felt good—not so good—as he felt on the evening that he received information that his sentence of death had been commuted to life imprisonment—but still good. He said he did..

And because he knew he had so many warm persistent friends upon the outside he was willing to receive a sentence of imprisonment in the state penitentiary instead of dangling at the end of a murderous rope ...

The article continued:

Davis arrived in Boise and to the prison by 4 o'clock sharp. As the Natatorium was passed he remarked on the elegant time he had there in the summer of 1895, when he first visited that resort. As he rode past the penitentiary gate in the hack up toward the institution he observed the condition of the orchard. He expressed great regret that so much of the fruit had been killed by the frost, but did see enough of the ripening peaches that there would be at least some fruit.

As he neared the penitentiary he caught sight of the new residence being constructed for the warden. Davis made a comment about the proper manner of constructing a handsome home, which he said he judged this would be when completed. The horse came to a stop and a number of employees were waiting to greet him.

Hello, Davis; how are you?" as he was greeted by Turnkey Charlie Chinn.

Hello, Charley, I am feeling first rate, and how are you and the rest of the boys?

Davis was escorted inside to the Warden John Hailey's office and after being processed he was taken to his cell on the upper deck of cell house in corridor B. He glanced about the cell and expressed satisfaction. A lamp and a towel had been provided. After a few moments in his cell he began a "levee." There are many prisoners there now who were acquainted with Jack when he was an inmate of the prison before this trip. They crowded about him exhibiting the greatest interest in his welfare and his movements since he has been away; Davis's eye had a scintillating twinkle—he was the lion of the day, and he was happy.

This would be Jack's home for the time being at least. Hawley's only hope was his last appeal to the Idaho Supreme Court, which was filed on April 25, 1901. This appeal would not be heard until the fall session.

Reconsideration (1901-2)

In April Hawley had appealed to the Idaho District Court in Cassia County for a new trial for Davis, based on new evidence being discovered since the original trial. Judge J.C. Rogers, the prosecuting attorney in the original trial, was now the district judge. Judge Rogers stepped aside and Judge Stewart sat in his place. Judge Stewart quickly ruled that the motion for a new trial had to be filed within 10 days of the trial in question. It was Judge Stewart's denial of a new trial that opened the way for Hawley to be able to appeal to the Idaho Supreme Court.

On December 4, 1901 the Idaho Supreme Court handed down a decision on that appeal. The court affirmed the order of the district judge in denying a motion for a new trial:

The District Court properly denied the motion. The application for a new trial must under the provisions of our penal code, section 7953, revised statutes, be made within10 days after verdict, unless the court or judge extends the time and then it must be made within the time so extended, else the application must be denied.

In all litigation both civil and criminal, controversies must at some time come to an end, and the judgments rendered by courts of competent jurisdiction settling actions or controversies between parties must, at some time, become a finality, hence our code provides, both in civil actions and in criminal actions, limited times in which motion for a new trial may be made in the trial court, and provides limited times within which court may be reviewed upon appeal, by the highest tribunal in the state.

The able and eloquent counsel (Hawley) for the appellant insists that under the provisions of our criminal laws, as they exist, in this state today, that "A" might be convicted of the crime of murder of "B" and sentenced to a term of imprisonment for life and one year afterwards "B" might turn up alive and walk into the court which tried and sentenced "A" and that court would be powerless to grant "A" a new trial. The contention of the able counsel is correct, but the picture which he presents is so overdrawn that there is no danger of its occurring one time in a thousand years.

Again, the case presented by this overdrawn picture presupposes the conviction of "A" without proof of the 'Corpus delicti—from Latin meaning "body of evidence" is the proof that a crime has taken place. When applied to a criminal case, proof of a crime must be shown in order to convict a person of a crime which could hardly occur in any civilized country. But in the event of such case, while the power to grant relief does not rest with the courts, yet our constitution has vested the power of granting relief to another tribunal, to wit, the board of pardons.

For the foregoing reasons the appeal from said order is dismissed, this court having no jurisdiction to reverse the order denying the new trial demanded.

Jack had already spent six months in his new home at the state penitentiary and, other than James Hawley appearing before the Idaho Supreme Court in late November on his behalf, nothing more was happening to obtain his freedom. The year 1901 was coming to a close and it would be nearly another year before there would be any more action.

The political climate in 1902, however, was changing in Idaho as well as across the nation.

The Silver Republican-Democrat coalition was swinging back to the Republican Party. Theodore Roosevelt would be elected president in 1904. In Idaho the current Democratic administration was in disfavor, particularly with the *Idaho Daily Statesman*. Governor Hunt along with Secretary of State Bassett had made the decision to seek re-election even with the tide obviously shifting to the Republicans. Attorney General Martin made the decision not to run for re-election. James Hawley himself was thinking about running for mayor of Boise. John Sparks was planning to run for governor of Nevada and made the decision to sell his cattle operation to the Utah Construction Company. The political situation would have made it an easy decision not to hold any more Board of Pardons meetings until after a new administration was elected in the fall. Hawley was continually communicating and passing information to Governor Hunt.

The Board of Pardons did announce that another meeting was scheduled for the fall term which would mean that meeting would actually be held after the election in November.

Hawley felt the opportunity was right to make another run at the board for a full pardon for Davis.

The Board scheduled a meeting for November 28, 1902. Hawley contacted Sparks advising him of his feelings and inviting him to submit an affidavit to the Pardons Board. By this time, Sparks was the governor-elect of Nevada, which obviously placed him in a somewhat different position than his previous appearance. Reading his deposition dated November 19, 1902, it is clear he was being very careful and precise in his statements.

Sparks laid out in detail his conversation with Bower on the morning of February 8, 1896 in his hotel in Ogden, Utah. Bower had gone to Reno a day or two after the incident at the sheep camp on February 4. Sparks explained that he had left Reno with a shipment of cattle to be delivered to Omaha and Chicago and had stopped in Ogden to rest and feed the cattle. While in his room at Ogden's Pacific Hotel, at about six o'clock a.m. he was awakened by James Bower. Sparks invited Bower into his room and noticed Bower seemed greatly worried and somewhat excited.

Sparks was very careful in explaining his position and duty after having become aware of the involvement of his superintendent in the affair:

I was greatly in doubt as to my duty in the matter. I regarded the statement made to me by Bower as the confidential utterance of a friend. I did not believe from the statement made that a crime had been committed, as the circumstances seemed to warrant Gray's apparent belief that his own life and Bower's life also were in danger when he fired the shots. I realized however, that there was great excitement in regard to the matter, and grave danger, therefore, if the parties were tried; I felt assured also, that if the matter became public it would ruin Bower and his family. Both Mr. Harrell and myself concluded, that the proper course to take was to keep silent as to our knowledge of the affair; not, however, with any intention of concealing the matter from the authorities, or of protecting any person charged with, or who had committed a crime, because I firmly intended if questioned by anyone who had authority so to do with reference to the matter, to make a full statement in regard to it. When Gleason and Davis were arrested in 1897 and charged with the murder of Wilson and Cummins, my proper course in the matter became a matter of still graver doubt with me. Both men had worked for my company, but outside of that I had no interest in either. I knew both of them were innocent, but could not make my knowledge public without violating the confidence that had been placed in me by Bower. Neither Bower nor Gray seemed willing to make public their connection with the affair. I did not believe it possible to convict innocent men, and was unwilling to betray the confidence of a friend unless it became my legal duty to impart my knowledge of the matter. I talked the matter over with Bower. He assured me that he would in the event of a conviction of either Davis or Gleason make the whole matter public; that he would never see an innocent man punished. I concluded my proper course was to defend the accused men. This Mr. Harrell and myself have continued to do from the inception of the case against Davis and Gleason up to the present time. I was not called as a witness at either trial, and informed no one, not even the attorneys for the defense, of my knowledge of the matter until after Mr. Bower had made his sworn statement, now on file, with reference to it ...

Judge O.W. Powers, one of the three prosecuting attorneys in the original Davis trial, sent another letter to the board reaffirming his current position and opinion that Davis should be pardoned.

In the matter of the application for a pardon for Jack Davis, sometimes called 'Diamond Field Jack', in addition to what I stated before the Board of Pardons at the time that his sentence was commuted, I desire to say that I have since then made considerable investigation of the matter and have learned what I could concerning the case and I am more convinced than ever that he should not have been convicted. In my opinion more than a reasonable doubt has been raised as to his guilt and I believe that justice demands his complete pardon for no man should suffer imprisonment unless his complete guilt is evident. Certainly in view of disclosures since his trial it cannot be truly said that his guilt is manifest.

Hawley also invited J.W. Dorsey, an attorney from San Francisco but previously a resident of Elko County, Nevada for a number of years, to participate in the appeal to the Board of Pardons. Dorsey had engaged in active practice in his profession for more than twenty-five years, had been the Elko County Attorney for two terms and for fourteen years had been employed in either the prosecution or defense of nearly every important criminal case tried in that county. Dorsey had worked with Hawley for several years on the Davis case, and affirmed, "I was employed in behalf of Jack Davis in the early part of 1899; and thereafter until July 1901, almost constantly. I was engaged either in the examination, preparation, or trial of some branch of the case, which involved the investigation of the facts; motions for a new trial; writs of habeas corpus; appeals, and applications for a pardon or commutation of sentence. I have repeatedly interviewed Jack Davis personally, and have heard his story from every point of view which my experience and desire to learn everything touching, or possibly bearing upon the question of his guilt or innocence, suggested."

He wrote about his familiarity with the range operation of the Sparks-Harrell cattle operation and the opportunity "to camp, hunt, ridden and driven with James E. Bower and Jeff D. Gray, and have heard each of them, over and over again, from every conceivable standpoint, on the witness stand in the crowded courtroom; in professional interview and under stress of the most searching and critical cross examination; in narrative form while hunting in the mountains and while along the public highways; in the presence of others, and in private interview, consultation and discussions; tell his story of the killing of John C. Wilson and Daniel Cummins."

Dorsey explained how he had carefully examined Buck Rice, J.P. Duncan, A.D. Norton, Henry Jones, C.H. Hewett and Henry Harris, on the subject of Jeff Gray's confession immediately after the killing, that he killed both Wilson and Cummins.

He had on several occasions discussed the question of the guilt or innocence of Jack Davis with John C. Rodgers, the district attorney of Cassia County, who filed the information against and had charge of the prosecution of Davis for the killing of Wilson. Rodgers had explained to him the reasons why he had first believed Davis guilty and how, after the conviction of Davis and after the admissions of Bower and Gray, he gradually grew more and more doubtful about Davis's guilt until finally, in light of the facts subsequently ascertained, he became convinced that Davis had nothing to do with the crime. Dorsey went on to say, "I have heard Judge O.C. Powers, who assisted Mr. Rodgers in the prosecution of Davis, and whose ripe experience in criminal cases and rare eloquence contributed largely towards the conviction, and how he now expressed the gravest doubts of the justice of Davis' conviction, and his absolute belief that Davis should not, and could not have been convicted, if Bower and Gray had come forward and testified at his trial to the facts subsequently admitted by them."

Dorsey made an interesting observation about his communications with Davis during this time:

I have received from him many letters embracing every phase of the inquiry—many of them of great length and of minute detail, one of them covering one hundred and twenty typewritten pages of legal cap when I had it copied. I do not believe that any man of the attainment and in the position of Davis could have said and written what he did to me and be guilty. I regard everything he has said and written as consistent with innocence and inconsistent with guilt. He has in every manner reviled Bower and Gray for their delay in confessing their connection with the killing of the sheepmen. I do not believe he would have dared to risk their enmity and abandonment if he were guilty. In my judgment he has been far too talkative and outspoken, too abusive of those of those whose withdrawal of support would leave him helpless, to have committed the crime charged against him. To my mind it is incredible that James E. Bower, well known and reputable citizen of Cassia County a man of property and standing in the community, who knows that a dominant industry in Cassia County is sheep raising, and that the sheepmen would probably constitute a majority of any jury that could be empanelled, and would be glad to find any reasonable ground for fastening guilt upon a cattleman, would have jeopardized his fortune, family and life for Jack Davis under any other circumstances than such as has been related by him, and it is impossible that Jeff Gray, between whom and Davis no friendship has ever existed; who was not even in the employ of Sparks-Harrell Company, would risk his life to save that of a man he scarcely knew and for whom he has no love. No other theory than that of implicit belief in the innocence of Davis could have enlisted the active sympathy and generous support of men like John Sparks and Andrew J. Harrell—men of highest character and position, one of them now the Governor-elect of the State of Nevada. Their personal knowledge of the character of the county over which Davis must have ridden if he had been a party to the homicide and the distance he must have covered within the time fixed by his known presence at various times on the range; their familiar acquaintance with Rice, Duncan, Norton, Jones, Hewett and Harris, and improbability that these men would attempt to falsely fasten the killing upon Gray (who was the brother in law of Jones, the employee of Norton, and who had worked for Hewett and with Harris, and was an old acquaintance of Duncan and Rice, and the friend of all of them); the long journey taken by Bower to find Mr. Sparks, immediately after the killing, and his confession to Sparks at Ogden, the moment he overtook him; the subsequent confession to Sparks—in short, their unbounded opportunities for getting at the facts and sifting out the truth; the fact that they were repositories of a secret which, during that period of intense feeling and bitter animosity, must be preserved, because it jeopardized the lives of two men—Bower and Gray; their unswerving belief in the innocence of Davis, and the loyal, disinterested and openhanded assistance which they have extended to him, have created, with the other facts and circumstances I have stated, a profound belief, to my mind of the strength and certainty of a mathematical demonstration—that Jack Davis had nothing whatever to do with the killing of Wilson and Cummins, or of either of them, by his own act, or by any sort of participation, conspiracy, foreknowledge or otherwise.

With a full understanding of all of the obligations of an oath, under the law of God and Man, I solemnly affirm that I believe Jack Davis is innocent of the crime for which he was tried and of which he was convicted, as I am, or as is any member of this Board of Pardons.

This plea from J.W. Dorsey was perhaps the most logical and persuasive of any testimony given during this hearing before the board. It continues:

The exhibits used at the trial, consisting of a cartridge shell, found near the wagon in which the killing for which Davis was convicted occurred and which was shown to have been fired by the person who did the killing; two bullets, a scrap of paper, and a corn-cob pipe were introduced in evidence before said board. Also a sack of .44 caliber cartridge shells, which had been presented by the prosecution before the Supreme Court of the State, also a package of .44, and .45 caliber shells shot out of .44 and .45 caliber revolvers by J.J. Plummer and L.R. Leeds, who were sworn and testified as to the result of the experiment were introduced on the behalf of applicant. It has been shown by the evidence on the trial of this cause that at the time of the killing the applicant, Davis, who carried a .45 caliber colt revolver was shooting out of it .44 caliber cartridges, and it was contented by the prosecution that the .44 caliber cartridge with which the murder was committed, was fired from a .45 caliber revolver.

The result of the experiment, as shown by both prosecution and the defense, demonstrated clearly in the judgment of the members of the Board that the .44 caliber shell found near the wagon where the killing occurred and introduced in evidence on the trial, had not been fired from a .45 caliber revolver.

After the reading of the affidavits Hawley presented his argument before the board. He called attention to the evidence formerly before the board and offered to be sworn so his statements might have the weight of testimony, as he desired to quote from the record. He stated that he forced Bower's confession to the murder of Wilson and Cummins and said he was able to prove that he obtained the confession only after weeks of effort on his part, following a deliberate step-by-step process. He offered to let the board examine his letter file and letter book showing the correspondence. He said such an examination would show the confession was not a prearranged affair.

Hawley continued his argument by pointing out the inconsistencies in the Cassia County District Court where Davis was convicted and where Fred Gleason was cleared based on the same evidence—this despite the fact that Gleason and Davis were shown to be together during the entire affair.

Considerable stress was laid upon the fact that no one appeared at this time to oppose the pardon, in contrast with the previous hearing.

Hawley pointed out how this indicated that the people of Cassia County had concluded the man was innocent. The only opposition, he said, came from a Boise newspaper and with a well simulated appearance of righteous indignation. Hawley proceeded to denounce *The Statesman* because of its role in helping to make successful the unholy conspiracy that brought about defeat of justice in the Davis case. He said: "It has continued this fight of its own volition in a contemptible course in that most contemptible newspaper in the state. I do not know how much it cost, but its course has been unfair and its statements untruthful."[20]

The only opposition presented at this hearing was a letter dated December 13, 1902 written by William Borah. In part it read:

To the Honorable Board of Pardons, Boise, Idaho

Gentlemen: Before the matter of the pardon of Jack Davis is passed upon, I desire that the Board be not misled by a report which seems to have been given credence by some and possibly all the members of the board—that is that all who were connected with the prosecution are satisfied now that Davis is innocent. It is but fair to say to the Board that this is wholly an error. It is quite true that some who were at one time excessive in their zeal to prosecute have been permitted to see new light and are quite excessive now in their zeal to release Mr. Davis. Knowing as I do the facts in the case and knowing as I do also that some of these men know them, I have no explanation to make with reference to this change of positions. I presume the charitable view to take of that matter is that they would rather see ninety and nine guilty men escape than to see one innocent man suffer (under certain circumstances).

I have not been connected with this matter professionally for a long time but I have kept up an interest in the case and have watched closely that testimony in the case, and I desire to say to the Board that I have not at this time one particle of doubt as to the fact that Jack Davis murdered Cummins and Wilson.

I am aware that I will likely be charged with prejudice and vindictiveness but I disclaim both. I simply know what I am talking about and I do not want it understood that the rumor that those connected with the prosecution have changed their views has any

---

20 Quotes taken from Y Board's Minutes and the *Idaho Statesman*.

verity in it so far as I am concerned. I am not going to review the evidence nor present any argument against this pardon, that is not the purpose of this letter, and all this has been gone over before. I submit this statement for what it is worth.

Very respectfully, William

The hearing adjourned the afternoon of November 28, 1902 and was submitted and taken under advisement by the board. They were scheduled to take up the case again on Monday, December 15, 1902. On Monday the case was set to be disposed of, but Governor Hunt said he was not yet ready and the matter went over until Tuesday. It did not get heard again on Tuesday and was put off until Wednesday, December 17th near the close of the state land board meeting, when the governor announced he was ready to take action in the pardon case. *The Statesman* reported the proceedings of the 17th in the next morning's edition.

The Board of Pardons thereupon convened and the matter was soon disposed of.

When the pardon matter was taken up there was some little discussion. Secretary of State Bassett said that he was favorable to a pardon. That had previously been known. The Governor indicated that he agreed with the secretary. Attorney General Martin then asked him if he was to understand that he was going to vote for a pardon. The Governor said that at the time of commutation in July, 1901, he believed Davis was guilty and that the showing made in his behalf before the board of pardons had been fixed up for the purpose. Since then, he said, he had become better acquainted with Mr. Sparks and had changed his mind.

There ensued a rather spirited scene, the Attorney General took occasion to express himself concerning the case, and some things of a pointed character were stated. The board then took a vote, resulting in Gov. Hunt and Secretary of State Bassett voting in favor and Attorney General voting against the pardon. Thus ended what has probably been the most stubbornly fought criminal case that the Northwest had ever known.

Davis was first notified of the action of the pardon board by Warden Ballard between 2 and 3 o'clock p.m. He was called into the warden's office, where Warden Ballard and Deputy Warden Fulton were seated. As he stood beside the warden's desk, Mr. Ballard said to him, "Jack, I received a message from Mr. Bassett, the Secretary of State, and he tells me the board has granted you a free pardon."

Davis stood still for a moment, and then his face was wreathed in a smile, but all he said was, "By Jove, that's good; I am mighty glad of it."

The warden and his deputy waited for Davis to say something else, but although greatly excited and much pleased, Davis said nothing further. The warden inquired if he had his citizen's clothes ready to don. Davis replied that only about ten days earlier they had been sent to the prison tailor to be cleaned and pressed, on permission from the deputy warden and captain of the yard Hunt (a brother of the Governor).

Learning this, the warden sent him back to the yard to don the clothes and pack his box, in preparation for leaving the prison. As soon as he entered the yard, Davis threw his hat up and called out, "It's all off, boys; I've got it!"

J. H. Hawley, his attorney, telephoned the penitentiary to tell them he would be there at about 3:45, and gave explicit instruction to the officials not to allow any newspaper reporter or others to talk to Davis before his arrival. When he arrived at the hour named, he went at once to Davis and cautioned him to say nothing and to refuse to make any statements to the reporters.

It was no surprise, then, that although visibly glad to be released, he made absolutely no statement when approached by reporters. The nearest he came to it was when he said, "I'm very glad to be released from imprisonment for a crime I never committed." And then he recovered himself and said nothing more.

In company with Ballard and Hawley, Davis started for the statehouse in a cab. They proceeded as far as the Natatorium when a stop was suggested, and the three went into the Natatorium bar. After several rounds of drinks, they proceeded on their journey.

Jack was taken to the State Capitol Building where he personally received his pardon from Secretary of State Bassett. The actual ceremony of giving Davis his formal pardon was very brief. The document had already been made out in duplicate and was lying on Secretary Bassett's table. Secretary of State Bassett was introduced to the prisoner, remarking as he shook hands that it was the first time he had ever met him. The two copies of the pardon were then passed to Davis and Warden Ballard, and the notorious criminal left for the city with his attorney, a free man at last.[21]

The next morning the expected reaction from the two Boise newspapers appeared in print. *The Idaho Statesman* editorial was predictable:

STATE DISGRACED!

The board of pardons has liberated "Diamond Field Jack" Davis. This result was not unexpected. For nearly two years it has been anticipated. Ever since the recklessness of the majority of the board was demonstrated, the public has been prepared for this pardon. It knew what influences were at work and with such a board, it did not seem possible that those influences would fail to bring about a result of this character.

Still there were a great many who hoped that this last disgrace would not be inflicted upon the state. The thought with these was that the exigencies of politics may have borne down the moral defenses of the majority of the board with respect to the other scandalous pardon of this administration and that with all political considerations removed, the board would stand firm against the insidious attempt to take this convict from the penitentiary. But that hope has been dashed to the ground, and the state bows its head, oppressed by a sense of outrage and disgrace.

Those who voted against the re-election of the governor and secretary of state will have additional cause when they read the story of the pardon of Jack Davis. All such will feel thankful that men of such acts will not continue to occupy high public positions.

Hawley had anticipated the *Statesman's* reaction but knew that the Democratic-leaning *Boise Evening Capital News* and *Idaho Capital*

21 The information describing Davis's release and events leading up the visit at the State House are taken from newspaper accounts.

News would give their support to the action of the board. Their report published December 18th reads in part as follows:

The organs opposing the present state administration seem to have only one argument—that a money influence is back of its every act. Of course, this is never proven, but it answers the purpose intended very well, that of sufficing in lieu of real reason for their opposition. This was the case when martial law was withdrawn from the Coeur d'Alene by Governor Hunt and later on, the occasion of the pardon of Paul Corcoran. Objector Martin joined with the opposition in both instances in predicting dire calamity and bloodshed, but the opposite effect was produced. Peace reigns in Coeur d'Alene and a prosperity so all-pervading on account of that act, that a big majority of the voters supported the republican ticket. After the usual howl over the Jack Davis case, the sober second thought of the people will probably approve the action taken. When a full hearing of the evidence was had before the board about 18 months ago resulting in a commutation of the death sentence, the dissenting member of the board expressed the conviction that there was no real evidence against Davis, except his own maudlin statements while drunk, that he was making $50 a month "shooting herders," that there was plenty of testimony showing that he could not have been nearer than 30 miles to the scene of the tragedy when it occurred.

But the Capital News_has no intention of defending the pardon on the evidence in the case; it is not a judge or jury, and it only presumes that the majority of the board weighed the evidence carefully. The crime was one of those incidents of stock range trouble when almost a state of war existed between the cattlemen and sheepmen over their respective grazing rights, and the real facts are more difficult to arrive at than ordinary murder cases, because of the fact that the parties to the conflict spent money lavishly, one side working for conviction and the other for acquittal. The only really good reason for the pardon of the defendant was the fact that after conflicting confessions and other new evidence had been injected into the case, the courts refused to grant a new trial because of legal technicalities, and this mass of accumulated evidence which was heard by the prison board was never passed upon by a jury and under the rulings never could be. Therefore, the only resource of the defendant was to the pardons board and upon that board necessarily devolved the responsibility of hearing and weighing the evidence in the case. There is no more fairness in assuming that their verdict was purchased than to accuse the average jury of being corrupted. It might be pointed out that they erred in judgment, but further than that, unless positive evidence is forthcoming, just and proper criticism cannot be pursued.

This man Davis upon evidence that Hon. J.C. Rogers, prosecuting attorney of the Fourth Judicial District, who conducted the case against him, and Judge O.W. Powers, one of the most eminent criminal lawyers in the West, who assisted in prosecuting him, and in their testimony before the prison board, now part of the state records, was so insufficient that they believe him innocent of the crime of which he was convicted and has been dragged from jail to penitentiary, according to the various phases of the case, in its tedious progress through the courts, and has lived through seven long years in the awful shadow of the scaffold. If he were merely a "bad man," convicted on "general principles," as too often the case, he has had a lesson severe enough to teach him the full value of good citizenship, and point the way to a future life of usefulness.

The first night of freedom for Davis was to be spent at the famous old hostelry, the Overland Hotel, where Davis had frequently stopped while engaged in "cow-punching" years earlier. On that night he was allowed to sleep without the restriction of lock and key for the first time in nearly seven years.

Davis was sentenced and re-sentenced to die three times and, in all, seven different courts affirmed the technical and trial procedures for his death sentence. During the six years Jack was incarcerated, his death sentence was suspended, reprieved, or stayed seven times, and finally commuted to life imprisonment before he was finally pardoned.

Asked about his feeling at these critical times, he said, "It would be impossible for me to tell you. A man never loses hope, though, until his wind is shut off. It was hope that kept me from breaking down. One day, 18 months ago, the sheriff in Albion could have hung me at any time during the day. It was that hour when my life depended on getting the message the relay riders brought from Minidoka that I was in the greatest suspense."

PART TWO

A New Life

Off to Nevada (1903)

When after six years of legal wrangling Jack Davis's "Ride to Freedom on a Slow Horse" came to an end, he boarded a fast train out of the state of Idaho. After he left the state, there is no known record suggesting he ever returned.

That marked the beginning of a journey to fame and fortune and, eventually, sinking all his money back into the ground seeking more riches only to end up broke and having to depend on his few remaining friends to put up the money to bury him.

But the remaining forty-six plus years of Jack Davis' life were adventurous and eventful. One might expect that after living in prison for six years nearly always under imminent threat of the death penalty, he might have focused simply on low risk and low visibility. But that was not Jack Davis' way; a psychologist would have had a field day to have been able to follow and study the man.

Davis stayed around Boise for a couple of nights before leaving it and the state of Idaho. Years later Katherine Bryan, daughter of Willis Sears, reported that Jack stopped in Albion for a short visit on his way to Salt Lake following his release from prison in Boise. Davis maintained a friendship and corresponded with Willis into the 1940s, according to his daughter.[22]

After stopping in Albion, Davis traveled on to Salt Lake, as *The Idaho Statesman* reported on November 21, 1904. There he visited with Judge Orlando Powers, one of the special prosecutors working with William Borah to convict Jack in the original trial. Since Powers had changed his mind about Davis' guilt and testified on his behalf before the Board of Pardons, Jack considered him a friend. Powers loaned Jack enough money to allow him to go to Reno and Carson

22 *South Idaho Press*, February 25, 1979.

City, Nevada. There he visited with Governor John Sparks, the man who had spent a small fortune on Jack's legal defense.

Davis' visit to Governor Sparks came at an opportune time. Nevada had experienced a major slowdown in mining activity for a number of years. The Comstock mine's production had been declining since the 1880's. But recent discoveries, around 1900, of gold and silver in the Tonopah area drew great attention not only in Nevada but from surrounding states as well. These discoveries were slow to develop into anything resembling major discoveries, but they had started to attract attention by the latter part of 1902, when more promising deposits of gold were being uncovered 26 miles south of Tonopah in an area to become known as the Goldfield District.

Present Day: Goldfield

Central in tracing and piecing together Jack's history after leaving Idaho is the story of the discovery of gold and the birth and decline of the Goldfield mining district in Goldfield, Nevada.

Driving south on Highway 95, passing through Tonopah and continuing south for 26 miles, you approach the top of a ridge, and an unexpected sight appears on the horizon. Within an isolated, somewhat barren terrain, what appears to be sizable city becomes visible. A number of two- and three-story brick buildings surround one large four-story hotel building. Homes spread out across the landscape giving the appearance of a good size city. Also on the skyline are several large churches with their spires reaching toward the clouds. Approaching the city you suddenly realize most of the buildings are vacant. Many of the homes are boarded up or have deteriorated to a skeletal framework. Most of the churches are still being used by the 300 or so people living in this almost empty city.

Goldfield is still the county seat of Esmeralda County and occupies the court house built in 1907 when the county seat was moved from Hawthorne. The presence of so many well preserved buildings along with the empty homes and commercial buildings indicates a once substantial city. It is sad, and eerie, to see what amounts to an abandoned city with a current population of only about 300 people living on the site of what was once the largest city in Nevada—a thriving city of 30,000 during the glory days, 1902-1910, of the gold rush era, with its lapsed promise of lasting wealth and prosperity.

I first contacted the Central Nevada Historical Society and Museum, located in Tonopah, and spoke to Eva LaRue, the assistant curator. After I explained to her what I was looking for, she offered to help me in my search. She said she would do a quick search for the name Jack Davis in their database. She called back in about twenty minutes and told me she was able to pull up his name numerous times in the short time she looked. I asked her if she thought it would be worth my time to make a trip to Tonopah and spend time researching. She thought considerably more information could be located, so I began making plans for the trip. Knowing that Jack Davis died in Las

Vegas and was buried there I had intended to travel to Las Vegas to find his gravesite, so now I had a double purpose for the journey.

Bert Stevenson, my good friend from Paul, Idaho, and I had already taken two trips down to northern Nevada looking at the area where the Sparks-Harrell ranches were located during the late 1880s. Most of the ranches, including their original homes and out buildings, remain in some state of repair and fun to visit. Bert gladly consented to join me for this latest search, a trip that would take three to four days in order to spend a little time looking over the new territory.

When we arrived at the museum Eva had the information she found laid out on a table in the library reading room. We spent a couple of hours reading and reviewing it, the majority from the old newspaper collection preserved in their archives and digital collection from around the state. Eva had on the table 75 different articles to review, and said if I wished to keep copies I could have them for the price of copying, which was $1.00 a copy. After reading through newspaper articles for several hours, I made the decision to have copies made and keep them for future reference.

Over several weeks following our visit Eva found more than 250 newspaper articles referencing "Diamondfield" Jack Davis. The largest collection of them came from twenty separate newspapers published in Nevada during the early 1900s. In addition to Nevada newspapers, a surprisingly large number of articles were published in California, Utah, Montana, the *St. Paul Globe* (Minnesota) and as far away as the *New York's Saturday Evening Post*. Judging from the number of newspaper articles over the years in these papers, journalists and the general public never lost interest and fascination with "Diamondfield" Jack Davis over his lifetime, long after his Idaho murder case was over.

My search for information included another trip to Nevada's historical society and archives in Carson City. The staff in Carson City was also enormously helpful.

In Goldfield (1903)

It is not clear when and why Davis made his decision to go to Nevada, and whether he was prompted by the news of the discovery of gold or if he went to visit his friend, Governor John Sparks in Reno.

It must have been the flurry of mining activity in and around the Tonopah area in 1902 and early 1903, and rumors of gold having been discovered just 26 miles to the south, that got Davis' attention and he must have shared the same excitement and anticipation as the hundreds of other men who had begun to stampede to the new discovery. Little detail is known about Jack's arrival in Nevada, but his notoriety apparently preceded him. On February 2, 1903 the *Reno Evening Gazette* published a short article in their paper:

"DIAMONDFIELD JACK"

Noted Character Here En Route for Tonopah Mining Camp.

Jack Davis, better known as Diamondfield Jack, the man who was sentenced to death twice in Idaho for the murder of a sheep herder on the range of Sparks & Harrell, and who finally had his sentence commuted to life, and was recently pardoned out, came in from the east Saturday and stopped off here to see his friend, Governor Sparks. He is en route to Tonopah. He says it seems good to be again at liberty. He went through something that few men could have withstood, and says that he knew from the start that he would never be hung for a murder of which he was innocent.

Twelve days later *The Tonopah Bonanza* newspaper reprinted a small article which *The Carson News* had printed earlier.

Gone to Tonopah

Jack Davis was a passenger south this morning on the V. & T. after spending the last week in Reno visiting friends He expects to follow mining in the new camp.

"Diamondfield Jack" has had several theatrical engagements offered him since his pardon and has received some very liberal offers from publishing companies to write a book, but he has declined them all. As Jack puts it: "I have been on the stage long enough and want to retire for a while."

These two articles were the first of many to come which noted his participation in the development of the gold district, as well as his enjoyment of the good fortunes of the gold rush boom in Goldfield.

Davis arrived in Tonopah in February with winter still making it difficult to spend much time out of doors. Just to go out and do prospecting in the hills required financial means and support; having proper camping equipment, food, and tools to survive would be an absolute necessity. Under the best of circumstances surviving in a desert environment during either winter or summer conditions is difficult and hazardous, particularly in isolated locations that are miles from any medical help.

It is not known who if anyone may have grubstaked Davis. We know Judge Powers gave Jack at least enough money to get to Reno. Governor Sparks may have given Jack the money to get to Tonopah and to immediately start prospecting for gold. Considering the amount the governor had spent on Davis' defense, it is conceivable that he could have grub staked him with a promise to be generously paid back later.

During the spring and summer of 1903 good deposits were being found but money necessary to develop the mines was not available. All of the miners knew that it took money to develop a strike. The size and possible value could not be known until sometimes extensive work and many thousands of dollars were invested. Most of the mining activity involved trading and selling claims, with a few individuals having the money to buy shares and in many cases total ownership for a few hundred or thousand dollars—or in many cases the equivalent of the cost of a meal. Stories abounded in which individuals sold their interests only to learn later that a few more feet of digging would have revealed instant riches. The major ownership and the operation of the larger mines fell into the hands of large mining companies or partnerships. The practice of leasing or bonding their claims to a better financed group or mining company was a practical solution for those not having the financial backing to buy the needed equipment and hire the manpower to develop their claims. Such conditions forced them to abandon their own operations and go to work for someone else, realizing they could now be working for the people to whom they leased or sold their claim for the price of a meal.

As early as August 1, 1903 and nearly two months before Goldfield City was organized, Jack's mining activity was reported in *The Tonopah Bonanza*: "'Diamondfield Jack' Davis and associates have thirty claims in the district on which they are doing assessment work. On a number of them good ledges are being opened up."

During the first few months that Jack was living in the Tonopah area he not only prospected for gold but also became owner of a building lot, which created a little excitement in the neighborhood. The first part of August 1903, Davis sold the building lot at the junction of South Main Street and Florence Avenue to a J.W. Davidson for the sum of $1,500. Davidson bought the lot with the intention of building a bakery on that corner.

On August 15, the Tonopah *Bonanza* reported on a conflict:

SENSATIONAL LOT JUMPING

The Triangular Lot on Main Street again Causes Controversy.

The contesting claimants for that triangular-shape piece of ground, situated at the intersection of Main and upper Main Street and Florence Avenue had an inning the early part of the week, and for a while it assumed a tragic aspect, but later quiet was restored and the participants are now moving along in the even tenor of their ways

The article continues: "The former occupant, W.B Sollender, claimed ownership, came upon the property, tore down the fence which Diamondfield had erected, and started to build him a house.

"Davis was out of town at the time, but when notified of the situation he immediately returned to town. He was on the property early in the morning when Sollender arrived to continue his building project. Davis was armed with a hatchet, prepared to start removing Sollender's previous day's work. Outsiders looked for blood, since Sollender had remarked the day before that he would win or die. As it turned out, he did neither. After a sharp exchange Sollender retreated, stating that for the time being he would quit. The Tonopah Mining Company settled the matter by issuing the deed to the property establishing Diamondfield proprietary rights to the ground. There were no further delays and the bakery was built."[23]

The activities surrounding Tonopah, and newly discovered gold just south of Tonopah were attracting hundreds of new people to the area, primarily men without families. Jack arrived early enough to be on the ground floor and he was considered a pioneer and one of the early recorded settlers. The town of Goldfield was born October 20, 1903, and according to Sally Zanjani, author of the book *Goldfield, The Last Gold Rush on the Western Frontier:* "Diamondfield Jack was present at the organizational meeting but was not one of the 36 signers of the organizing resolution creating the Goldfield mining district and naming the town."[24]

The city of Goldfield was bursting with activity which reflected a full-fledged gold rush. Initially most of the newcomers were prospectors seeking gold but often they ran out of money or luck, or simply found a better opportunity by going to work in the mines or even starting up their own little business such as mercantile, restaurants, shoe repair, barber shops, or the one priority business which nearly superseded the importance even eating or sleeping establishments—a saloon. The Goldfield building boom lasted for three to four years and resulted in 49 saloons, 27 restaurants, 15 barber shops, 6 bakeries, 22 hotels, 84 attorneys, 17 doctors and 10 undertakers.[25]

The sudden influx of individuals from all walks of life and from all corners of the country inevitably brought the usual human problems. Several newspapers sprang up with plenty of stories for the locals to read, stories about the miners' successes, failures, mishaps, and family gossip and other domestic issues.

In any boom town, entertainment businesses follow the money. Usually saloons would be some of the first businesses to open, followed by dance halls, theaters, men's clubs, women's clubs, lodges, and bands. Predictably, brothels prospered in Goldfield. As the

---

23 *Tonopah Bonanza*, August 15, 1903.

24 Page 27 of Sally's book *Goldfield, The last Gold Rush on the Western Frontier*.

25 Facts taken from *Goldfield Historic Walking Tour Booklet*, November 2009 3rd edition.

population continued to increase, Goldfield became a center for business as well as entertainment, gaining national prominence as a result of the presence of a man named C.L. "Tex" Rickard.

Rickard was an entertainment promoter in Goldfield and brought national attention to town when he brought the lightweight championship bout between Joe Gans and Battling Nelson to Goldfield on September 3, 1906. An outdoor arena was built with a ring and a large area of bleachers that could accommodate the 6,200 spectators. The city of approximately 30,000 was overrun with fans as well as the national media covering the championship fight. The media was trying to report the fight by telephone, telegraph, and the written word. The contest still holds the record as the longest lasting prize fight on record. It lasted forty two rounds and took two hours and 50 minutes. The gate receipts were $76,000, the largest for a prize fight up to that time.

"Tex" Rickard was responsible for a number of other productions in Goldfield which gained him national attention, later earning him the position of manager of the Madison State Gardens in New York City during the 1920s.

Jack was present and busy with his land ownership, prospecting, and mine development activities in and around Goldfield during this time. Sometime in the latter part of 1903 Jack was known to have presented to James Ford, a stable owner, a check for $21,000 and a large share of stock in return for the loan of an old mule named Maud which he used during his prospecting trip to Goldfield in the autumn of 1903.[26]

Ford was named a few months later as one of the owners of a claim upon which a gold strike of fabulous richness was made by the lessees of the claim. The other owners listed were "Diamondfield Jack", Dan Spaiding, and W.H. O'Neil, manager of the Nye County Mercantile Company. It is not clear whether James Ford's involvement in this claim was part of the stock mentioned in the above paragraph or if just a partnership arrangement with some local businessmen. Over the next couple of years Davis continued to remember and be very generous to those who helped him along the way.

The year 1904 was a busy one for Davis. Besides being involved in a number of different partnerships, he built himself a new home in Goldfield and laid out the new townsite named Diamondfield. Laying

---

26 Page 41 in *Goldfield, the last Gold Rush on the Western Frontier.*

out a new townsite meant selling the lots, and building another home for his bride-to-be in Diamondfield. Jack invited two friends from his Albion jail days, Willis Sears and Charles Krise to come to Goldfield to work with him. Davis also established a new stock brokerage and real estate firm with Willis Sears as the manager, and gave a gift of appreciation to Judge Powers from Salt Lake City, for testifying before the board of pardons.

Not least among his 1904 activities, he got married.

After leaving Idaho, news about Jack Davis was slow getting back to Boise. The first news that filtered back to Boise was a reprint of an article from an Oregon newspaper. On January 8, 1904, a little over 12 months following his December 17, 1902 pardon and departure from Idaho, the *Baker City Herald*, at Baker City, Oregon published an article which the *Idaho Statesman* reprinted in part:

HE HAS STRUCK IT RICH: "DIAMONDFIELD JACK" DAVIS WINS FORTUNE'S SMILE

Jack Davis, famous throughout the west as "Diamondfield Jack", after a strenuous career as a border fighter, diamond detective and a convicted murderer under sentence of death, struck it rich in Goldfield district near Tonopah, Nevada.

Davis is now possessor of a number of claims of exceeding rich ore. He has been at work in the Tonopah district at mining ever since his pardon about a year ago.

Any mention of "Diamondfield Jack" brings to mind the greatest criminal case in Southern Idaho, if not the entire West, in which he was the central figure. Viewed in light of the present day, one is filled with wonder at the evidence upon which he was convicted. The conviction speaks wonders for the district attorney who conducted the trial and also shows how little average jurymen consider evidence in rendering a verdict.

The Herald expresses the hope that the reports of his lucky strike are true and that "Diamondfield Jack" will live long and enjoy his prosperity.

About the same time *The Tonopah Miner* reported on January 23, 1904: "On the Red Butte Jack Davis, Van Spaulding, and White Wolf & Company have a good ledge at a depth of 20 feet. J.P. Harvey took an option on this property this week."

On February 6, 1904 the *Tonopah Bonanza* ran a special article describing the excitement and activity happening in the Goldfield District.

The short time Goldfield has existed someone returning for a visit would be surprised at the number of gold producing claims in a short period of time. To go through the Combination mine, pan the free gold that comes from ledges wider than the shafts and drifts—see the smelter returns which shows that much of it goes better than $300 per ton—then to the Jumbo mine and see more big ledges of medium grade ore with some shoots going from $275 to $1467 per ton—then four and one half miles northeast to where Kane and McMahon, Jas P. Harvey and Patsy Clark, and "Diamondfield Jack", Dr. White Wolf and associates having opened up big ledges of ore on their different group of claims, which is identical with that of the Combination and runs better for the same depth—then across country to Kane Springs, eight miles east of Goldfield where you would see free gold visible to the naked eye.

One of the old-timers said, "We offered interests in our claims when we were hard up a few months ago for almost nothing and they wouldn't believe we had anything here. Now they are offering us ten and a hundred times as much, but when we get our properties opened up a little more, we will prove that even the prices they are offering now are not a tenth of the value."

The original owner of the Florence had many claims but no money. He offered it for $40 but was refused, and finally succeeded in getting the location work done and recorded. It is needless to say that an offer of $40,000 for the Florence today would not bring forth even a pleasant smile.

New prospectors arrived daily in the new district, but there were no hotels to accommodate them, and only a few hastily constructed rough lumber boarding houses and eating establishments had sprung up with attached tents serving as kitchens and dining rooms. Men were using canvas tarps as the roof of dugouts burrowed into hillsides, or any other available material as coverings to provide some protection from the weather. With the backdrop of barren hills, clumps of sage brush and a scattering of yucca trees, the scene was the sight of a dismal and bare existence.

Davis spent a considerable amount of his time prospecting four or five miles northeast of Goldfield and located and developed several good-producing mines. Due to the number of mines being developed in that vicinity he made the decision to lay out a city to accommodate them. The biggest producing claims at the time were the Red Butte and the Daisy Group of claims referred to in the above news article. Jack was part of both of those groups.

The town site of Diamondfield, named in honor of and by Jack Davis, was laid out during February, 1904 about four miles northeast of Goldfield. An application was also made for a post office for the city of Diamondfield, with a Mrs. Rose Campbell as post-mistress. The day after completion of the survey for the new town, eighty-seven lots were sold, including every lot on Main Street. The day the lots were being sold a large number of men were at work clearing sagebrush from the streets, and lumber was already stacked on lots, ready to start construction on new buildings. The Diamondfield Townsite Company, of which Frank M. Ish was the manager, incorporated to furnish the town and mill with water from a couple of springs two miles from town. By December of 1904 Davis had a well dug and a reservoir to supply the town with its needed water for domestic use. The little town, Diamondfield, never grew in population to more than 300 souls but it did give Jack recognition and status in that section of Nevada. He was elected mayor of the city, and he was the owner and lessor of several mines in the vicinity.

Jack had already started to build himself a house in Goldfield early in February of 1904. It is unclear whether or not the picture credited to be Jack's house is the one he later built in his town of Diamondfield or the home he built and maintained in Goldfield.

The March 12, 1904 edition of the *Tonopah Miner* reported:

Close to the town of Diamondfield, very rich ore was uncovered in what was described as Red Butte No.1. The owners were Dr. White

Wolf and "Diamondfield" Jack Davis. Eight feet of ore was opened up and panning shows particles of gold a large as pinheads. During the same period of time Governor Sparks, T.L. Oddie and Jack were reported to have bonded a group of claims from Mr. Riggie and Gunter. It was reported these claims were about one quarter of a mile south of the Black Butte, a rich producing mine also near the town of Diamondfield, and good values were recovered from the surface of the ground.

DIAMONDFIELD JACK'S HOUSE IN DIAMONDFIELD E. W. Darrah

Jack Davis' house in Diamondfield. (photo from newspaper article)

During the next few years Governor Sparks' name was associated with Davis in several ventures. Jack maintained a good working relationship with the governor and his family through the years in Goldfield and many years following. In 1916 the *Idaho Statesman* reported that Davis and Spark's son, Charles, developed a copper mine together near Needles, California.

In that last transaction, the name Tasker L. Oddie was listed as an associate of Davis. During the next few years, Tasker Oddie was named in a number of mining ventures with Jack. Oddie was one of a number of individuals to make a fortune during the 1906 silver boom in the Tonopah region. As a twenty-seven-year-old man he traveled out west from New Jersey to work in the Nevada mines. He earned his law degree in night school but had never practiced law. Having the law degree gave him the opportunity to work part-time as the deputy county recorder in Belmont, Nye County, as well as acting as a defense lawyer for a few clients. This proved to be the right opportunity at the right time in his life. During this period of time Oddie became acquainted and had several dealings with Jim Butler, the acting district attorney for Nye County, a local rancher and weekend prospector. Jim came into possession of some high grade ore samples from an area south of Belmont in what was to become Tonopah, resulting in a silver boom that rivaled the Comstock strike at Virginia City some 40 years earlier, or at least raised hopes of such. Jim Butler offered Tasker a quarter interest in the claims if he would pay and arrange for the assaying of the ore as the mine properties were developed. This venture resulted in Tasker making a fortune over the next couple of years. When the gold rush moved down at Goldfield Tasker invested some of his money in good gold producing property. Unfortunately, he fell into the same trap as many of the miners who sometimes made large fortunes in a short time. By 1907 Tasker had invested his fortune back into the ground seeking a new bonanza strike, which too often leaves the once-wealthy broke.

Tasker had better luck in the political world. He ran for, and won, first, Nye County District Attorney (1902), then the State Senate (1905-1909), then Governor in 1911-1915, and finally the United States Senate for Nevada (1921-1933).[27]

During March of 1904, *The Tonopah Miner* mentioned Jack in several of their columns about all the mining activity in the area.

"Diamondfield Jack" Davis came over from Diamondfield last Saturday and returned Sunday. Jack is full of business these days.

"Diamondfield Jack" Davis has bonded the Estella Villa claims, halfway between Diamondfield and Klondike, to Walker Brothers of Salt Lake City. Fritz Swartz, a friend from Idaho, Sam Wingfield and others went out Thursday to do location work, and will establish what will be known as Tognmoi camp.

---

27 Information about Tasker Oddie is from the book (*Letters from the Nevada Frontier*, by William A. Douglas and Robert A Nylen.

A man well acquainted with the mining camps around the State stated he felt the Goldfield Mining District offered more promise than any in the state. His name was Ben Pearlman and he had taken an option on four claims from "Diamondfield Jack" Davis and associates. This group adjoined the Red Rock group, which was under bond to T. L. Oddie and others.

"Diamondfield Jack" Davis bought an interest in the Louis way's lease and will sink a 50 foot, timber and crosscut. Very rich ore was encountered in the Red Butte No. 1 early in the week by the owners, Dr. White Wolf and Diamondfield Jack Davis and expect to be shipping within a few weeks. The lease to Jim Harvey continued to develop good ore. He currently has three shifts working. The shaft is down sixty feet and has gone through thirty feet of ore and is drifting both ways with the face showing good values.[28]

In April Jack was known to open a silver and lead mine operation at South Klondike, located 16 miles south from Tonopah. The South Klondike region was in the silver and lead district, similar to the Jim Butler mines further north near Tonopah. It was reported to have a three-foot ledge with values running $90 a ton. Located east of the Klondike property, Jack bonded to the Walker Bros of Salt Lake City the Estella Villa Claims. The Walker Bros had been very successful in the merchant trade and the mining businesses in Utah.

Jack was busy not only in his business ventures, but was pursuing his domestic life during 1904. On May 20, 1904, *The Goldfield News* announced his marriage: "'Diamondfield Jack' Davis, in whose honor the town of Diamondfield was named, was married in Tonopah last week Wednesday evening to Mrs. Minnie Williams. The ceremony was performed by Judge Lindsey, after which a beautiful supper was enjoyed by the guests at the Merchants' Hotel. Mr. and Mrs. Davis are now at their new home in Diamondfield."

Three additional newspapers included the announcement of Jack's marriage in their community sections. *The Tonopah Miner* made the following announcement:

Diamondfield Jack Gets Married.

---

28 *Tonopah Miner*, Mar 12, 1904.

Jack Davis, Diamondfield mining magnate, was married on Wednesday evening to Mrs. Minnie Williams. The wedding ceremony took place at Smith's Lodging house, on upper Main Street, Justice Lindsay officiating. After the ceremony the wedding party repaired to the Merchants' Café where a sumptuous repast was served. The guests were Mrs. William Smith, Miss Bianca, Miss Maud Williams, Mr. Milas Robinson and Mr. Ed Clark. Mr. and Mrs. Davis will reside in Diamondfield.[29]

The *San Francisco Call* newspaper carried the marriage news, as did a number of other papers, but added as a postscript; "Cupid brings happiness to the stirring life of a turbulent frontiersman! Twice within the shadow of the gallows, then a prospector and now a mining magnate, "Diamondfield Jack" Davis now has taken unto himself a bride. According to advice from Tonopah, Mrs. Minnie Williams of that city has become his wife. Now "Diamondfield Jack", once a cowboy, next a doomed convict, then a poor prospector, is a mining magnate and now a happy husband."

Jack's marital status did not remain stable for long. In the years after their marriage, the newspaper made occasional mention about Mrs. Minnie Davis's travels and visits. She made several trips to San Francisco for what appeared to be medical reasons, and on one occasion she was noted to be in better health upon her return. In April of 1906 she was reported to have recently returned from Sacramento, California where she would purchase a house, but the paper included no explanation or reason why she would be buying a house in Sacramento.

Jack and Minnie were married for five years. On January 7, 1909, *The Goldfield Daily Tribune* printed a story reporting that Jack Davis was being sued by his wife for a divorce. She claimed that he had deserted her and failed to properly provide, and claimed that he was threatening to sell all his property to cheat her out of it. The article said the proceedings came as a complete surprise to friends of the pioneer. Her claim also stated that following their marriage in1904 Jack had all kinds of money and prospects. Mrs. Davis informed the court that through their joint efforts her husband amassed a great deal of mining claims, stocks, money, and real estate in Goldfield, Diamondfield, and

29 *Tonopah Miner,* May 21, 1904.

other sections of the state. She claimed that he had already disposed of some of his holdings, and said he would clean it all out and force her upon the charity of her friends.[30]

In her petition for divorce, Mrs. Davis asked for an injunction to restrain Davis from selling or mortgaging any of his property, and for her share thereof. She also requested alimony *pendente lite* (contingent upon the determination of pending lawsuit) and finally an absolute divorce. It is clear that she had a very good attorney working for her.

As Davis prospered he did not forget his friends from his Idaho experience. Over the years a number of instances are recorded in which Jack gave gifts or made offers to people involved with his prison days in Idaho. One of the notable cases involved Willis Sears and Charley Krise, from Albion. Willis and Charley were both involved in carrying the Board of Pardon's telegram that gave Jack a reprieve from the July 3, 1900 hanging date. The sheriff had been informed of the pending reprieve on July 2 but had to wait for the telegram verifying that the board had in fact granted the reprieve. Willis and Charlie waited at the train station in Minidoka for the telegram's arrival and then the two of them rode, (by two separate routes) copies of the telegram in hand, the thirty miles by horseback to Albion just hours before Jack's scheduled hanging.

The March 5, 1904 issue of *The Tonopah Miner* tells of Diamondfield's gratitude to Willis and Charley: "Willis Sears, an old friend of Diamondfield Jack Davis, is now making his home with Jack, and Charley Krise, another friend, is expected here shortly. The two made a ride from Minidoka to Albion carrying the reprieve from the Board of Pardons which stayed the execution of Jack and now that Jack is making a fortune in Goldfield mines he has invited his old friends to come and share his prosperity."

According to reports both Willis and Charlie worked for Jack in his mining business for some time. No information was available as to how long and what Charlie may have been doing for Jack during his stay in Goldfield, but there is information about Willis indicating he remained in Goldfield for several years before returning to Albion.

According to Willis's daughter, Katherine Bryan, Willis worked for Jack in Goldfield and Diamondfield for two and a half years before returning to Albion, where he lived out his life. She remembers her

30 Details concerning Jack's divorce in the Goldfield *Daily Tribune* dated Jan. 7, 1907.

father talking about Jack and their close friendship over many years into the 1940s. She also said that while her father was in Nevada working with Jack he made enough of a stake to return to Albion and purchase the Sears homestead and enough cattle to start a ranch. He later became the postmaster in Albion and retained that position for 35 years. Katherine Bryan remembers her father talking about his experiences with Jack and keeping up a correspondence with him for years.

Later in 1904, the *Goldfield News* announced:

New Brokerage Firm With Willis Sears

"Diamondfield Jack" Davis and Willis Sears have entered into partnership and will do a general brokerage and real estate business at Diamondfield. Jack is one of the pioneers of the district and is probably the best posted man on the section around Diamondfield. In his business dealings he has gained the reputation of always keeping his word and this will stand him in good stead in his new business. Willis Sears is an old friend and has made many friends since coming to Goldfield.[31]

In November of 1904 came another instance of Jack showing his gratitude to a friend, this time to Judge Orlando W. Powers from Salt Lake City. *The Salt Lake Herald* broke a story about Jack giving a valuable gift to Powers.

"DIAMONDFIELD JACK DAVIS MAKES VALUABLE GIFT TO JUDGE POWERS"

Salt Lake Attorney the Recipient of mining Stock Worth $10,000- Had Assisted in Prosecuting Davis for Murder but Worked Hard to Secure His Pardon – Also assisted Davis Financially After his Release from Prison.

"Diamondfield Jack" Jack Davis, the central figure in one of the most remarkable criminal cases on record, has given the man who drew his death warrant at Albion, Idaho six years ago, mining stock valued at $10,000, says the Salt Lake Herald. Judge O.W. Powers of

31 *Goldfield News*, Oct 21, 1904.

Salt Lake is the recipient of the gift. Judge Powers with William. E. Borah of Idaho, assisted the state in prosecuting "Diamondfield Jack" for murder, secured a conviction and by order of Judge Stockslager, drew Davis' death warrant.

Afterwards having been convinced of Davis' innocence, Judge Powers appeared voluntarily before the Idaho Board of Pardon to urge that Davis be released. This was done about two years ago. Davis came to Salt Lake penniless, Judge Powers loaned him money enough to get to Tonopah Nev., and Davis departed with the promise that he would repay the money. Since then Davis has prospered. As one of the original locators of the famous claims at Goldfield and Diamondfield, he secured large holdings in the camps, changed his ways of living and is said to be a leader of the law and order element in the mining section where he resides.

Recently Judge Powers received a letter from the Secretary of the Diamondfield Gold Mining Company enclosing 2500 shares of stock with the statement that it was the personal gift of Davis.

1904 was in fact a very successful year for Jack.

Besides laying out a new townsite, resulting in the sale of a considerable number of lots, forming several profitable partnerships in gold, silver, and lead mining, and getting married and becoming a happy husband, Davis closed out the year with two more notable accomplishments. One was completion of the community well to provide domestic water for the residents of the town named in his honor. The second was the announcement on December 31 that Governor Sparks had appointed Jack, mayor of Diamondfield, to represent Nevada at the National Livestock Convention to be held in Denver, Colorado.

That convention was to begin on January 10, 1905, but he was unable to attend the convention due to an illness that confined him to his bed for several days. He was up and around on the 10th but by then it was too late to start on his trip to Denver. The illness left him looking pale and thin but he was soon able to resume his business activities.

1905 started, as 1904 had ended, with news of new strikes being made all over the gold districts. The prospectors were fanning out in all directions from Goldfield, eager to locate new strikes.

The *Goldfield News* reported a major strike in a new district in the Kawich Mountains. The new district was named Goldreed. It was located 60 miles east of Goldfield and 30 miles south of Reveille. The Goldreed Mining Company owned about 40 claims in the new Goldreed District, with some claims showing very rich ledges with rocks showing gold which could be seen from quite a distance with the naked eye. Rocks could be broken off and the gold could be seen well distributed through the rock, with assays going from $24 to $500 per ton; break-even price was said to be around $22 per ton.

The *Goldfield News* continued its report of the week's activities in the new Goldreed district:

"Diamondfield Jack Davis went out this week with associates and located 25 or 30 claims. He also located a town site, two miles this side of the big strike, and will send out men at once to sink a well for water."[32]

A week later Jack sent an outfit over to Kawich; included in the party were surveyors to lay out the new townsite, and workmen to sink wells in two places. Jack had much confidence in the new district.[33]

Another fascinating character surfaced about this time.

His name was Arthur V. Buel (1877-1952) and he has been described as Nevada's most prolific editorial cartoonist. His long newspaper career started in the mining towns in the Yukon Territory, and eventually he ended up in Tonopah Nevada in 1905, attracted by the new boom. While working in Tonopah he honed his distinctive approach to the art of caricature. Buel took a job with the *Tonopah Sun*, where over the next three years he immersed himself in the social and political life of communities in central Nevada. His pen-and-ink drawings offered up a steady line of often bitter visual tirades, complete with equally bitter captions, against politicians with whom he or his editor had differences of opinion. He would equally portray his target in a good light when he agreed with the individual or issue.

Buel utilized several stock devices in his cartoons. His subjects most often had large heads and small bodies, a technique that allowed the artist to exaggerate the facial features of his targets. Every drawing that Buel penned included a prospector's burro in the lower corner, a

32 *Goldfield News*, January 6, 1905.

33 *Tonopah Miner*, January 21, 1905.

stubborn little protagonist to act as Buel's (or his editor's) alter ego, often asking prickly questions about current political matters.[34]

One of his first cartoons for the paper was directed at Jack Davis, a cartoon appearing in the paper dated on April 16, 1905. The information written below the cartoon was not any kind of tirade against Jack but rather was complimentary towards him.

One with the name and fame of Mammon-build gold camps is "Diamondfield Jack." His has been a strenuous life, regard which The Sun has no exact data. Its artist, Arthur V. Buel having sketched Mr. Davis on the sly while he was negotiating a mining deal, got the picture truer to life than a posed photograph. It is known, however, that "Diamondfield Jack" is a true borderite, having punched cattle from the canyons of the muddy Colorado to the continuous wood where rolls the Oregon. He has had every experience that could come to the man who sings by the campfire. " I want free life and I want fresh air, and I sign for the canter after the cattle, the crack of whips like shot in battle, the medley of hoofs and horns and head, that wars and wringer and scatters and spreads, the green beneath and above, and dash and danger and life and love."

"Diamondfield Jack" was three times in the shadow of the gallows, convicted of murder, and no red mark under the ear, for a heart that eats as warm and true as Jack's knew the cowboy was innocent-John Sparks, Nevada's cowboy Governor, a man who transacts no business on the anniversary of the fall of the Alamo, ex-Texas ranger, Indian fighter and true square American-came to the rescue and said to the Board of Pardon: "Diamondfield Jack" is as innocent, gentleman, as are you. Give him his freedom."

Thus came the subject of this sketch and he in his daily walk and conversation proven true the word of Governor John Sparks. "No man stands higher in the estimation of Diamondfield, Goldfield and Tonopah than Jack Davis, ex cowboy and now mining king.[35]

---

34 Jim McCormick, Arthur Burl-Biography of a Nevada Caricaturist.

35 *Tonopah Sun*, April 16, 1905.

Buels' first characterization of Davis. (from Tonopah Sun, *1905)*

Davis would be the subject of another of Arthur Buel's cartoons during the I.W.W. strike against the mine owners in March 1907. Jack's personal involvement in this conflict was the subject of several newspaper articles.

Davis branched out from mining and real estate into transportation during the spring of 1905. On May 20, 1905, the *Tonopah Bonanza* reported: "Jack Davis, Mayor of Diamondfield, has established a one day stage line between Goldfield and Bullfrog and is doing a rushing business. His line makes the jaunt in ten hours."[36]

36 *Tonopah Bonanza,* May 20, 1905.

Jack was known to be prepared. (from Tonopah Sun*)*

Six weeks later another announcement said: "Diamondfield Jack Davis has sold his interest in the stage line between Goldfield, Beatty and Rhyolite to Egan & Stetson. The father of Chas. Egan planned to put $10,000 into the line for improvement. Mr. Egan Sr. is banking on his son's knowledge of mining as well as from the stage business, to get returns. Jack Davis still retains his interest in the Stage line from Tonopah to Goldfield."[37]

His involvement in the traffic business was noted in the papers once again early the next year. A January 1906 article said, "Diamondfield Jack Davis has gone into the traffic business between Tonopah and Manhattan and to accommodate the crowds he has put his big omnibus auto, which formerly ran between Columbia, Goldfield, and Diamondfield, into commission. The Auto is making a round trip a day between the points, covering 120 miles and is loaded to its fullest capacity on every trip."[38]

Sometime in late May 1905, Jack's wife Minnie attracted public attention. Jack took her to San Francisco for medical treatment where she underwent two operations and remained several months to recover.

---

37 *Beatty Bullfrog Miner*, May 20, 1905.

38 *Goldfield Review*, January 18, 1906.

She traveled from San Francisco back to Tonopah on August 12 before returning to their home in Diamondfield.[39]

While Davis was in San Francisco with his wife, he was busy promoting the gold districts. "In San Francisco and all other places I visited," he was quoted as saying, "all the talk among mining men is Goldfield. I saw people from all over the country and I got tired answering questions in regard to the camp. I predict that there will be 60,000 people in the district—actual residents—within the next three years. All will not live in the metropolis of the district as it is our intention to make Diamondfield a city also."[40]

While Minnie was in San Francisco recovering from her illnesses, Davis made several trips between Goldfield and San Francisco attending to business. During this period of time while Minnie was ill, Davis was attempting to develop a major high grade ore strike in the Diamondfield-Triangle mine, of which he was the general manager. To extract the ore from the required deposits, a gasoline-operated hoist was badly needed by the crew. The trips Jack Davis made to attend to his wife gave him the opportunity to locate the hoist and have it shipped to the mine.

Controversy was no stranger to Jack in his many business activities while in the gold fields of Nevada. One incident, reported in the paper, occurred soon after Jack returned to Goldfield after spending five weeks in San Francisco. On returning to Goldfield he went to view a new strike near the Triangle, one of his own mines.

The *Goldfield Review* reported, "The new strike was on the Gold Coin claim, belonging to Jumbo Mining Company. The difficulty arose over the exact position of a side line between the Gold Coin and the Triangle claim belonging to Davis. Davis claimed the new strike was really on the Triangle. To back up his statement he pointed out the places from which the survey stakes had been removed and placed at their new location. It is understood that the Jumbo Extension Company admits that the stakes were changed but exhibits a quitclaim deed supposedly from Davis to the disputed ground, which covers an area

39 *Goldfield News*, June 16, 1905 and the *Tonopah Bonanza*, August 12, 1905.

40 *Goldfield News*, June 16, 1905.

about 100 feet wide and the width of the Gold Coin claim. Davis repudiates this deed and there is promise of bitter law suit over it."[41]

There was no further mention of this incident until six months later when on December 15 *The Tonopah Daily Sun* reported the story, framing it in terms of an old-fashioned frontier shootout. The article starts:

Judge Bell is busily studying Nye and Esmeralda county maps to determine in which county the dispute ground is situated so that should a real old-fashioned frontier shooting scrape occur he will know whether it will fall upon his duty as acting coroner to gather up the corpses or whether it will fall upon the shoulders of the coroner of Nye County.

The controversy was still over the position of the side line between the Gold Coin claim and the Triangle claim. The story runs to the effect that Davis yesterday appeared on the scene with a posse of men and ordered the LaFoe and Dougherty lessees off from their workings. They obtained their mining privileges from the Jumbo Extension people and Davis claims that a recent and accurate survey shows they are out on his Triangle ground.

In point of fact the lessees' shaft is within thirty feet of Davis' shaft and it was previously understood that the boundary line ran between the two. Not so now, however, as Davis claims that the Extension ground overlaps him 135 feet. At the time he ordered them off he is alleged to have stated: "I'm willing to give you boys a lease on this ground, but it must be understood that it is on my ground, and not the Jumbo Extension's."

The dispute carried over onto the streets of Goldfield when Major Duncan E. Harrison, who owns an interest in the lease, met T.G. Lockhart, one of the large owners in the Jumbo Extension ground on Main Street. They did not address each other in any complimentary terms and the bystanders for a time thought there would be a fistic encounter.

Major, in an argument with B. Lind, another large owner, over the telephone, had a misunderstanding in which Lind is alleged to have used some very forcible language. However this may be can-not be

41 *Goldfield Review*, June 29, 1905.

ascertained, but at any rate it ended by Major's swearing out a warrant for Lind's arrest for using abusive language.

Both Messrs Lind and Lockhart are men of highest integrity and have never been known to be aggressive in trouble of any kind. Mr. Lind declares the whole thing is an attempt to blackmail the Jumbo Extension out of a portion of its ground and his company will be able to show the intruders up in anything put in proper light.[42]

The fallout from all this is unclear. The only follow-up to this dispute can be gleaned from a February 16, 1906 article:

"DIAMONDFIELD TRIANGLE HAS A RECORD STRIKE

ASSAYS SHOW IT TO BE THE GREATEST EVER MADE UPON THAT FAMOUS PROPERTY

The largest and most important strike *ever made on the Triangle mine at Diamondfield was reported yesterday by Diamondfield Jack Davis, who brought some of it to Goldfield to have assayed. The results were surprising to him.*

At the bottom of a winze at the 100-foot level a seven-foot vein of ore was uncovered which looked exceedingly good. The average assay obtained from the 7 feet was $30, while about a foot of it returned the valuation of $100 and a few cents.

The owners are going to it with two shifts and propose putting on another as soon as it is demonstrated that the vein shows indications of not pinching.

This discovery is of more than the ordinary significance, as it demonstrates that the vein, which has been supposed to exist in that vicinity, has been found and will add value to the other properties in the district.

The famous Gold Coin Mine, that has produced such fabulous values, adjoins the Triangle, and the leasers who now have it are as pleased with the new strike as are the Triangle people.[43]

---

42 *Tonopah Daily Sun.* December 15, 1905.

43 *Goldfield Daily Sun,* February 12, 1906.

After the boundary dispute in December over the Gold Coin Mine overlapping the property of the Triangle, a settlement apparently occurred, as indicated by the mention of a new leaser of the property. There is no indication whether it was leased from The Jumbo Extension or from Jack Davis.

Another incident was reported within the same month. This incident involved claim jumping but resulted in two court actions. In the first, two individuals, C. E. Southworth and W. D. Frey, had charged Davis with pulling a firearm on them when he ordered them off the claim they were working on. Davis claimed it was not he but one of his associates who pulled the firearm. In the justice court at Beatty, Nevada and after a trial, Davis was released from the bonds he had been required to post to keep the peace against those individuals. Three separate witnesses each swore that Jack did not draw a gun when he ordered Southworth and Frey off the Confidence claim. The case was dismissed.

Both parties stipulated that their civil rights involving the title to the properties in dispute should not be considered at this trial. This question was left pending in the United States court.[44]

The second action came about two weeks later and involved the legal ownership of the property. The newspaper reported, "Evidently Frey and Southworth were jumpers, as at the trial of Davis at Beatty on last Saturday he was discharged by Judge Sexton after a lengthy trial, where both side were represented by Counsel. Mr. Davis said, 'I think that my action in driving these men off my ground will end jumping in the Bullfrog District.'"[45]

"DIAMONDFIELD JACK" DAVIS HITS THE TRAIL

NOTED WESTERN GENTLEMAN WITH A BLOODLY RECORD
Is Now a Mining King of Nevada and is Worth Anywhere From Forty Cents To Million Dollars

"Diamondfield Jack" Davis, penniless and nearly friendless, migrated to Nevada. He struck the desert state just at the time—the time of the opening of Tonopah and Goldfield. Not satisfied with the ragged edges of those camps, he started one of his own, 'Diamondfield

44 *Beatty Bullfrog Miner*. July 1, 1905.

45 *Tonopah Bonanza*, July 15, 1905.

City'. He sold many town lots, and made a great deal of money in that way. Also he went into mines. He is now rated as a King."[46]

In 1906 Davis, the former convicted murderer, fulfilled his civic duty serving in the district court as a jury man. The case involved three officials, including a Judge Bell, being charged with calling about fifty women into the Justice Court on the 25th of January, 1905 on a charge not contained in any statute book: "Maliciously running a house of prostitution."

The women were forced to pay fines for this offense. The accused officials contended that the fines collected were regular and that in cases where the defendant women did not appear they were represented in court by persons acting as their attorneys; but the excess over the fines remitted to the county was legitimate.[47]

The big strike at the Triangle Mine reported by Davis back in February was drawing attention from some of the large mine operators and stock speculators. *The Goldfield Daily Sun* reported:

The general talk is that William Douglas, the big Tonopah mining man is trying to secure a controlling interest in the property and has offered a large sum of money for a specific amount of the stock.

Some of the rumors state that Diamondfield Jack Davis has been offered 22 ½ cents per share for all of his stock and upon taking into consideration that the stock is being offered in the open market around 11 cents, the closing of a deal of this kind means big doings as regards a general rise in the stock as soon as public announcement is made that the deal completed.[48]

In April Jack embarked on a new venture and a slightly new concept in the local mining community. "Jack, as firm believer in the future prosperity of Southern Nevada, is the organizer and promoter of two new mining companies. One is in the Manhattan district and the

---

46 *Idaho Statesman*, July 15, 1905.

47 *Goldfield Daily Sun*, February 21, 1906.

48 *Goldfield Daily Sun*, March 7, 1906.

other adjoining the Quartzite claim near Diamondfield. The latter company comprises forty acres and it is his intention to conduct systematic development work from the very start. It is termed the Quartzite Annex Mining Company with J. P. Marshall, cashier of the Nye and Ormsby County Bank as secretary and treasurer.

The other company is the Manhattan Elk Gold Company and comprises seventy-five acres, otherwise six locations some of which are in the heart of Manhattan Mining district. Connected with him in this enterprise are Arthur G. Raycraft, Manager of the Nye and Ormsby Bank in Tonopah, and Richard Raycraft."[49]

A week later: "Jack has a force of men engaged in development of the forty-acre estate of Quartzite Annex Mining Company with a number of ledge outcrops uncovered showing they will make into pay grade at depth."[50]

Davis' business involvements continued to expand outside mining in April of 1906. He purchased the Hot Springs Resort, located five miles northeast of Beatty (which is approximately 60 miles south of Goldfield).

HOT SPRINGS SOLD; THE FAMOUS RESORT WILL BE GREATLY IMPROVED

G. F. Hicks has sold his hot springs, five miles northeast of Beatty, to Jack Davis for a large consideration. About $800 has been paid down and Davis will soon take possession and improve the property. A large Hotel will be erected and the plunge enlarged. Money will be freely spent to make it an attractive resort. A road will be built to it from Transvaal so that it will become a half-way house between Beatty and the new gold camp.[51]

How successful was Jack Davis during this period?

One of the most notable commentaries on Jack Davis and his place in the mining world of Nevada is found in a publication titled *SUCCESSFUL AMERICAN: Portraits and Biographies of Prominent Engineers, Miners and Business Men of Nevada*. The contents for the

49 *Goldfield Review*, April 5, 1906.

50 *Tonopah Miner*, April 21, 1906.

51 *Beatty Bullfrog Miner*, April 21, 1906.

August 1906 publication included biographies of twenty-four men ranging from mining company presidents, a surveyor, mine managers, a stockbroker, a mining lawyer, the discoverer of the first located mine in Goldfield, and "Diamondfield Jack" Davis," Cowboy Millionaire and Practical Miner, Goldfield. The article read in part:

One of the richest and most generous-hearted of Nevada's Miners—His Romantic Life.

One of the most prominent figures in the discovery of the richest veins of ore in the Goldfield District is "Diamondfield Jack" Davis, founder of the town in his honor, and whose life has been surrounded by a combination of circumstances as sensational and dramatic as any ever conjured up in the imaginative mind of the writers of the wildest fiction.

The article continues, with a brief outline of his early life in the saddle on the plains of Western Texas and onto the cattle range of Idaho:

Where he was arrested, tried and sentenced to be hanged for a murder of which he was wrongfully accused. But the proof of his innocence would have come too late had it not been for the quick action of two of his friends and former companions, Willis Sears and Charles Krise. Soon thereafter the true state of facts bearing upon the case was placed before the Board of Pardons, and those who help to convict, now lent their aid to securing a full Pardon, and "Jack" Davis returned to his friends a free man.

Besides his many interest in Diamondfield and Goldfield, Davis is a large holder of properties in Bullfrog, Kawich, Lida, Manhattan and other districts, many of which promise him rich reward. Among the properties in which he is largely interested are the Diamondfield Black Butte Mining Company, the Goldfield Skylark Mining Company, Diamond Bullfrog Mining Company, and last but by no means least, Diamondfield Triangle Mining Company, which has several good claims within half mile of the town of Diamondfield.

One of Mr. Davis' characteristics is his loyalty to his friends, among whom he numbers governor of the State, its U. S. Senators and *prominent citizens. To Mr. J. I. Ford, who had grub-staked him in 1903, Mr. Davis presented a half interest in one of his claims which afterwards sold for twenty-five thousand dollars. He also duly remembered Willie Sears and Charlie Krise, who had risked their lives to save his when under sentence of death, on the wild ride from Minidoka to Albion, and he not only repaid General S. Nixon, who had loaned Mr. Davis $1500 at a time of greatest need, but presented him with fifty thousand dollars' worth of stock in one of his companies.*

In closing it is but justice to add that Mr. Davis' word is as good as his bond, and those who do business with him invariably get a good deal.

Cartoon by Arthur Buel following newsboy incident.

Adversaries (1906)

The fall of 1906 marked the beginning of serious labor problems in the new gold districts in Central Nevada.

The trouble started when the Industrial Workers of the World (IWW) called for a strike against the mine owners and initiated a boycott aimed at the merchants and newspapers. The boycott attempted to keep union members as well as union sympathizers from patronizing the stores or buying any newspapers carrying ads for the merchants. It was an attempt to encourage the local businesses to put pressure on the mine owners to make a settlement. The IWW also attempted to have other unions in the city join by calling their own strike against their employers. The union attempted to shut down not only the mines but the entire city, and they succeeded in scaring a few merchants from buying ads in the local newspapers.

When the other unions, including the Typographical Union, refused to strike or join the boycott against the merchants and newspapers, a backlash against the IWW quickly developed. Two members of the Typographical Union, employees of the *Goldfield Sun*, were being followed by a mob led by Joseph Smith, business agent of the labor organization. The mob followed them along Main Street, calling them scabs and pelting them with rotten fruit. Two members of the mob who were intoxicated struck at the boys. Finally, the two boys took refuge in Diamondfield Jack's office on Ramsey Street, eliciting an interesting reaction from Jack.

The Tonopah *Bonanza* reported: "The two boys took refuge in Jack's office and locked the door. The mob gathered a thousand strong. "Diamondfield" appeared on the scene and upon learning the nature of the trouble, drew a couple of guns from his pocket and chased the bunch half a block down the street. At the Nixon corner an officer demanded his guns. "Diamondfield" declared he would kill the first man who attempted to disarm him. Smith, the leader of the mob, beat everybody in the getaway. A hundred influential people have called at the Sun office to assure the management of their support, and a further demonstration on the part of Smith's followers will surely precipitate trouble."[52]

On the same date in the same paper another article was published describing the situation with the union down in Goldfield.

According to latest advices from Goldfield excitement still prevails over the Industrial Workers of the World situation. The mine owners have determined to break the boycott of the Industrial Workers of the World on the local newspapers. George Wingfield and "Diamondfield" Jack are selling papers on the street with the members of the Carpenters' Union and Trades Council.

The action arose from the attempt of the I. W. W to force the carpenters to join the organization. When they refused they declared the carpenters could not work at the mines. The men went to George Wingfield, who said if the carpenters did not work neither could the miners, intimating that he would close down all the mines he controlled rather than be forced to yield.

Carriers attempting to sell the newspapers on the street Wednesday were attacked by a mob of 300. "Diamondfield" Jack with two guns routed the mob without firing a shot, as stated elsewhere in this issue. Wingfield came to Tonopah, gathered a number of determined influential men (four automobile loads) and returned to Goldfield ready for battle with the agitators. He took arms and is prepared for serious conflict.[53]

This story was carried by a number of newspapers around the county, including the *Idaho Statesman* and the *New York Evening Post*. Each story carried some variations.

The September 13, 1906 *Idaho Statesman* article was written as a dispatch from Goldfield.

DIAMONDFIELD JACK ROUTS MOB AT GOLDFIELD

The I. W. W. (Industrial Worker of the World) adherents in this camp began a desperate attack on three carriers selling the Goldfield

52 *Tonopah Bonanza*. September 8, 1906.

53 *Tonopah Bonanza*, September 8, 1906.

Sun on the streets here last night and for a time it looked as though serious trouble would result. "Diamondfield" Jack Davis appeared on the scene, however, and singlehandedly routed a mob of 300 or more."

The carriers, all I. T. U. printers, (International Telegraph Union), undertook to sell papers on the streets and when they had gone some distance from the office of the Sun they were set upon by a mob of I. W. W. sympathizers and forced to flee. One made his escape and was rescued by Manager Payne, and the others were chased to the office of "Diamondfield Jack" Davis, where they sought refuge. The mob started to follow them in, but Mr. Davis is not accustomed to allow any such proceedings on his premises, and drawing a pair of moral suasionists in the shape of heavy Colt's revolvers, he started to ascertain the cause of the trouble. By the time he reached the door the gallant 300 were in full and hasty flight.

The correspondent of the New York Evening Post told the story about the mob action with a few trimmings to make the story a little more interesting. Relating the instance at Goldfield, as well as a few facts about Jack's colorful past experiences in Idaho, the New York Evening Post correspondent introduced some features not in the record, showing how stories of that kind become magnified and embellished as they roll along. The correspondent reported:

DIAMONDFIELD JACK DAVIS AT GOLDFIELD

STORY OF HIS DEFENSE OF NEWSBOYS FROM MOB.

Some weeks ago "Diamondfield Jack" Davis distinguished himself at Goldfield by defending some newsboys against an attack of a mob of anarchists who were intending to beat them for selling the Sun, a paper that had been boycotted.

On the day after the prize-fight the merchants and mine operators of Goldfield decided that it was time for them to disregard the boycott of the I. W. W. and they assured the proprietors of both the Goldfield and Tonopah papers that they would renew their patronage. At the same time the union men awoke to the fact that their organization was about to be demolished. They passed a resolution calling upon all the members of the union to mob any men or boys who attempted to sell the Goldfield Sun on the streets.

The sun was just dipping down behind the ridge of barren hills that circle the mining camp when four young men set out to peddle the newspaper. They had journeyed about 300 feet from the little printing office on the main street, when half hundred I. W. W. men charged upon them. The boys fled in the direction of the brokerage office of "Diamondfield Jack," and bolted through the door with the union mob at their heels.

As the men lumbered up to the door the broker stepped out and presented two weapons of extraordinary size.

"I'll give you until I count 3 to beat it", he said slowly, waving the long barrels of the revolvers at the mob. The men scattered wildly before he had counted "three," and in the span of a few seconds the entire street was clear.

It was not the weapon that Davis displayed that counted so much. His reputation as a "bad man" and a "terror" has a great moral force in Goldfield. He was thrice sentence to be hanged in Idaho for the murder of two members of the I. W. W. Ex-Gov. Hunt pardoned him and the reprieve was brought to him in a spectacular manner.

The hanging was scheduled for the early afternoon in a small, desolate county seat 30 miles from the railroad. United States Senator Nixon of Nevada, by whom "Diamondfield Jack" had once been employed, had interceded with the governor and finally obtained a pardon, early on the morning set for the execution. When the state authorities endeavored to telegraph a reprieve, however, they found that the wires had been cut by Davis's enemies. Thereupon, it was necessary to get the reprieve to the condemned man by relays of ponies. The noose was about his neck when the state's messenger arrived.

Davis has always contended that members of the I. W. W. cut the wires and his bitterness towards the union is only natural. During the early stages of the boycott against the Goldfield and Tonopah newspapers he was in San Francisco. Immediately he arrived in Goldfield and learned of the situation, he announced his intention of breaking the union, and volunteered his services as a newsboy for the Goldfield Sun. He had also organized the mine operators and miners against the union, and notified Joseph Smith, secretary of the I. W. W., that he and his walking delegates would soon "be run out of town.[54]

54 Article reprinted in the *Idaho Statesman* on October 9, 1906.

Obviously the "facts" added in by the writer were clearly not in the record, but they did make the story more interesting for the New York readers.

The trouble between the union and the mine owner subsided for several months following the confrontations during the newspaper boycott.

Both the union and the mine owners continued to fight for their respective positions. Increased wages and improved benefits for the union members riled the mine owners while the constant effort to increase profits put more pressure on the miners. The biggest agitation between the two was the practice of high grading by the miners. High grading was the miners taking high grade gold ore out of the mine for their own profit. The high grade ore would be removed from the mine in their lunch boxes, pockets or any means they could think up. A market to sell the ore in small quantities appeared in the form of illegal assay companies willing to buy the stolen gold from the miners. In order to the combat the practice the mine owners attempted to set up change-rooms requiring the miners to change from working clothes into street clothes under close inspection conditions by mine security. This practice was offensive to honest miners and resisted by the union. The mine owners determined the practice was costing them thousands of dollars.

One case of interest has been recorded in the book authored by C. Elizabeth Raymond. The author reported a case where George Wingfield suspected a shipment of stolen or high graded ore being shipped out on a train to Reno and then on to an assay company in Vallejo, California. Wingfield wired ahead to Reno for legal assistance in recovering the sacks of ore upon their arrival in Reno. He then took the same train to Reno as the shipment of ore. Upon arriving in Sparks, Nevada, Wingfield left the train and raced to Reno by automobile where he met the sheriff at the train station and took possession of the ore. They had the shipment transferred to the Nixon National Bank for safe keeping while giving notice that his replevin suit against Wells Fargo & Co was merely the opening salvo in an ongoing effort to crack down on a generally accepted practice of stealing ore.[55]

---

55 C. Elizabeth Raymond's book titled *George Wingfield, Owner and Operator of Nevada* pages 68 and 69.

Contentions and accusations continued to increase with neither side willing to compromise. The IWW made an attempt to force the Carpenters Union to join with them, and to enforce their demand called the carpenters' helper off the job, then ordered grocers, water men, and restaurants not to sell to carpenters. On March 6, 1906 the Miners Union served notice on the Goldfield Consolidated Mine Co. that they would strike unless all workers around the mines (including the carpenters) became members of the Miners' Union. The company refused and the miner's representative called his men off from the Mohawk. The next day when the men returned to work they found themselves locked out.[56]

Davis' name continued to appear in the local newspapers whenever reports were printed about new gold strikes or existing mines being expanded and developed. Jack was also involved in the civic activities of the communities. In the September 1906 Esmeralda County Democratic convention Jack Davis was honored with a nomination to the county central committee, a position he did win.[57]

During November of 1906 several reports went out about rich strikes at the Diamondfield Triangle Mine.

The work of prospecting the ground is under the eagle eye of the best mining engineer that ever came into camp in the person of H.E. Peterson, who has been appointed general manager of the company by the new board of directors. Under the management of Diamondfield Jack it was proven that the sixty odd acres owned by the company contained good bodies of shipping ore. Davis was so busy with other propositions that he paid very little attention to the Triangle. Since the opening up of the big body of high grade ore in the Detch and Brewer lease and also in the company's workings by the Daisy syndicate, adjoining the Triangle, it has again come into prominence.

The Mohawk mine during this period of time was mining extremely high grade ore which was producing upwards of $50,000 per day. The company had just installed 8 new drill compressors and with these new compressors they will expect to double their production.

---

56 *George Wingfield, Owner and Operator of Nevada*, pages 70 and 71.

57 *Idaho Statesman*, September 13, 1906.

Just as the news was going to press last week, five masked highwaymen walked into the shaft house and compelled the top men to throw up their hands. The engineer was ordered to break open a locker where there stored seven sacks of high grade that were probably worth $1000 each. The ore was taken down to the wagon road some 100 feet from the shaft house and loaded into a wagon and then driven away.

Manager Hays was promptly notified about the robbery. He looked around a little to see if he could locate the ore, and having failed, went quietly to work with the remark: "What is the use of worrying over a little thing like? There is more of that stuff below, and more than we can hoist."

That carload of high grade is going to be shipped. The estimated value of it is placed at $1,000,000. The ore will average $25,000 a ton. [58]

On November 10, 1906, *The Idaho Statesman* reported on several Idahoans having interests in gold mines in Goldfield. Names mentioned included "W.C. Dewey, son of Colonel Dewey of Silver City fame and the Dewey Palace in Nampa, M.E. Hopkins, J.H. Hutchinson, and ex-Governor Hunt, the signer of Jack Davis's pardon in 1902."

The big news coming out of Goldfield in November of 1906 was the passing of ex-Governor Hunt while working in Goldfield with the other men from Idaho. It is not clear just what connection they had with Jack Davis, but references were made connecting Jack in a partnership with W.C. Dewey on two leases on claims in the Goldfield area.

The *Idaho Statesman* reprinted the special dispatch from Goldfield:

Ex-Gov. Hunt passed away in Goldfield on November 25th following a recurrence of pneumonia. His death makes vivid the fact that here on the desert with 40 bodies in the morgue tonight, there is another side in the scramble for hidden gold here near Death Valley. When one leaves loved ones in the beautiful valley of Payette and Boise and comes here where every green thing has a thistle and every creeping thing a sting, he leaves much. Gold is here but death goes with it.

58 *Tonopah Miner,* November 3,1906.

One of the saddest events of the funeral was the grief of Diamondfield Jack Davis. He had never met Governor Hunt until the Governor came to Nevada. Like Jean Val Jean, Jack Davis had redeemed himself here. His grief today was pitiable.[59]

Jack's business reputation in and around Goldfield seemed to be in good standing, particularly with the local newspapers. It is the job of the newspapers to expose or point out irregularities in communities, but there didn't seem to be many incidents in Jack's years in Nevada reported in any paper.

The most complimentary article written about Jack was in the *Goldfield Gossip*, a newspaper that printed its purpose in each edition, a purpose that seems to include investigative and public protection aspects: "It is GOSSIP'S aim to carry the advertisements of those firms only that carefully select the stocks they promote. We wish to make the pages of 'GOSSIP' the best guide possible to the buyers of stock."

The *Gossip*'s February 1907 article about Jack Davis reads:

It has been said of Southern Nevada mining that it draws too greatly upon the purse of the public, and that mine owners are less inclined to spend their own money than that of other people.

There is a man in Goldfield whom half the world knows as Diamondfield Jack Davis, who is absolutely free from this charge that today after spending two or three fortunes in the development of his numerous properties it is hard to keep him back from putting every dollar of his own money into work that should be paid for by the companies with which he is concerned.

In other words, and this so unique a characteristic in the mining game that we must dwell on it a little, if a stock company is formed upon one of the Davis properties, the problem before A. K. Wheeler, who is Davis' business partner under the firm name of Davis-Wheeler Company, is NOT how to make Davis rich, but how to keep him from making himself poor; how to keep him from putting his own money into ground that belongs to the company and not to individual Jack Davis.

---

59 * *Idaho Statesman*, November 26, 1906.

You will admit that this fact is interesting, and unusual. It means a good deal to "Gossip" public to know that Jack is a splendid type of a man.

We have told you always in buying promotion stock or treasury stock to look for the man who is the heaviest stockholder and find out something of his character.

We bank on Jack Davis, and guarantee him straight all through. His mining record is the best in camp, bar none.

For this reason we guarantee the offering of the treasury stock of the Daisy Wonder, which is Davis' property, to be the best buy in that camp at the price, 30 cents.[60]

Davis' reputation in west-central Nevada seemed to be good through these years, based on the newspaper articles of the time.

Only one of Jack's personal letters was found in the archives we searched. Dated December 18, 1912, it was written to newly elected U.S. Nevada Senator Key Pittman, a statement of support from Davis, who was a former mine partner. Other than that one letter, Davis' history in the area is traceable through newspaper articles written by twenty-one separate central Nevada newspapers, reporting on Jack's personal and business matters, for evidence about his character. The Tonopah and Goldfield papers wrote numerous articles over the years Jack resided in those two cities, but few were anything but favorable.

On March 17, 1907, the *Los Angeles Herald* published a special Mining Edition featuring "Diamondfield Jack" Davis with a picture of Jack standing in front of one of his mines. Under the picture the caption reads, "Under the management of Diamondfield Jack, this mine produced $700,000 the first year—rich ore stacked for shipment." Stacked around Jack are several hundred sacks of ore. The special edition included three full pages of written material and pictures of the town of Diamondfield, plus a full page telling about Jack's contributions in the new Bullfrog district. One page includes a large dignified photo of Jack in suit and tie, titled "JACK DAVIS, MAN OF ACTION" with wording below the picture reading: "Thrilling Career, Teeming with Generous Deeds, Sanguinary Struggles and Final Success—Now in Command of Diamondfield Mining District"

60 *Goldfield Gossip*, February 2, 1907.

Four days before the *Los Angeles Herald* article was published, a local restaurant owner was shot by two union representatives. The trouble between the IWW and the community of Goldfield had not disappeared after the 1906 strike and boycott. The conflict erupted again on March 10, 1907 when the two union activists shot and killed at point blank range the local restaurant keeper, John Silva, while he stood in front of his restaurant. There had been an argument over Silva's hiring of nonunion employees. It culminated in the shooting, witnessed by a number of local citizens, including Jack Davis: "Without a warrant for arrest, having recognized the killer, Jack and four other men went to the home of the perpetrator, made a citizen's arrest and delivered him to the sheriff."[61]

This action by Jack resulted in a series of retaliations aimed at him over the ensuing years, the first attempt occurring just a couple nights after the shooting of the restaurant keeper.

The union agitators promised further trouble following the arrest of their two members, Joseph Smith and Morrie Preston, for the murder of Silva the restaurant owner. "The threat prompted one hundred citizens to be sworn in as deputies to stand guard over the city. There was fear that they might try to burn the city."[62]

A wild scene ensued on the corner of the ally just back of the Nixon bank at about 10:30 p. m. Jack was one of the leaders of the determined men who were taking every precaution to prevent violence to the city, and on that night he was standing guard at that intersection. As John Cook, the banker, crossed the alley, one of the agitators took a shot in the dark at either Cook or Davis, who was standing on the corner where the alley joins Main Street. The bullet passed between the two of them and no one was injured, even though a number of people were in the area at the time.

Jack quickly whirled around and fire two shots down the alley in hopes of winging the would-be assassin. Efforts were made to find the man who fired the shots, but to no avail.

The next day the *Tonopah Daily Sun* ran a cartoon by Arthur Buel depicting Jack's reaction over the shooting event.[63]

61 Testimony from Preston and Smith trial on April 19, 1907.

62 *Salt Lake Tribune*, March 25, 1907.

63 *Tonopah Daily Sun*, March 13, 1907.

The trial for the two men accused of killing the restaurant keeper began on April 19, 1907, just a little over a month after the killing. This same thing happen in the Idaho trial of Jack Davis and, as with Davis's trial, the short time between the arrest and the trial became an issue in the ensuing years. Jack served as one of the chief witnesses for the prosecution in the trial. During the trial it was revealed that the union had developed a hit list which included, among others names, John Silva and Jack Davis. Testimony from that trial indicated that in a meeting at the union hall, Smith was asked why Silva had not been killed yet. The next day Smith did shoot him. At the same meeting, $250 was offered to anyone who would kill Diamondfield Jack Davis.[64]

The IWW's dislike of Jack Davis followed him for a number of years. Trouble with the union continued to worsen until Governor Sparks called upon President Roosevelt to send in troops to protect life and property of the mine owners as well as homes and buildings of the city's merchants.

One day while the soldiers were standing guard, Jack was walking with an officer when an agitator approached them and started to direct some insulting remarks to them. The man appeared to have been drinking and kept up with the insults, refusing to leave. "Jack at once engaged the man in a rough and tumble fight, during which more kicking than fighting was done by the agitator. Jack was able to restrain the man until an officer came and intervened, but before any weapons could be brought into play a deputy intervened and succeeded in separating the combatants".[65]

In late 1908 the mine owners and the Goldfield Local Miners Union 220 reached some agreements, but still the relationship was strained. An agreement was reached to reduce the wages scale by 20 percent and at the same time reduce the cost of living also by 20 percent. The mine owners agreed not to hire any members of the Local Union 226 of the Western Federation of Miners. The union also agreed to have state troopers positioned near the mines to protect life and property.

On another front, the *Tonopah Daily Sun* ran a short article:

LIFE OF GOLDFIELD GIRL THREATENED

---

64 *Tonopah Daily Sun*, April 25, 1907.

65 *Goldfield Chronicle*, December 9, 1907.

GOLDFIELD, December 14—Fearing that threats against her will be executed, Margaret Shea, a stenographer, sought protection of Franston. She received a letter saying, "Account of the remarks made by you against the union men, and for your loyalty and friendship for "Diamondfield Jack" Davis, you are warned that unless you leave this camp within a week you will be shot down in the streets like a dog."[66]

66 *Tonopah Daily Sun*, December 14, 1907.

Running into trouble (1908)

On March 17, 1908 the *Goldfield Daily Tribune* reported Jack running into trouble up in the town of Rawhide while escorting a party of 'Frisco Brokers viewing some of Jack's properties.

Jack Davis and Party jailed in Rawhide.

The greatest sensation was created today, when it was known that Jack Davis was arrested in this peaceful burg. When it is understood that Davis went through the wars of Goldfield, and the latter had coddled him into the belief that he was a public benefactor, the crowd around the post office refused to believe that anyone had the temerity to make an arrest in such a case. Jack was not alone but went to the pen with a bunch of 'Frisco brokers whom he had brought into camp to look at his promotion. They had been pretty free around town, when five deputies, who got wind of their armament, rounded them up in a bunch and told them to throw up their hand. They were then all led down to the detention house. It was thought by some that the arrests were entirely due to the actions of the Western Federation of Miners of Goldfield, who wanted to vent their spleen on Jack Davis for his activities in the labor troubles.[67]

The charge against Davis was carrying concealed weapons, and the news reverberated across the state and into the state capitol building. Jack sent a telegram to Governor Sparks dated March16, Rawhide.

Gov. John Sparks

"Rangers are needed here to supersede the county officers. Four deputy sheriffs last night made an attempt to murder me, and would have done so had I not been with a party of friends.

---

67 *Goldfield Daily Tribune*, March 17, 1908.

We were going to the hotel when set upon by the deputy sheriffs. They used vile language and tried to force us to an overt act. A conspiracy to murder at whose instigation you can guess. I had a permit to carry arms, but they ignored it. Had to lay in Jail all night although the officers were offered $10,000 cash bond. Dozens would endorse this but fear for their lives."

Jack Davis

Governor Sparks responded by ordering the Nevada State Police to the scene of trouble immediately. The *Reno Evening Gazette* reported the incident with big headlines:

STATE POLICE TO BE ORDERED TO RAWHIDE

Capt. Cox, superintendent of the State Police, stated that he had intended to send a number of state police to Rawhide this week but now the trouble had happened he will rush them to that point. It had been reported a number of union agitators from Goldfield had moved to Rawhide and trouble was expected."[68]

This incident resulted in injunctions being issued from the federal court at Carson for President McKinnon of the Goldfield Miners Union and forty-nine other members of that union, restraining them from interfering in any way with the operations of the mines.[69]

On March 28, 1908 the *Nevada State Journal* reported that "Diamondfield Jack" Davis, who was arrested a few days ago at Rawhide on a charge of carrying concealed weapons, was tried before a jury in the Justice Court at the place, found guilty and fined $100. He at once gave notice of an appeal."

His next news appearance was in a cleverly-written article from the *Goldfield Chronicle* in May of 1908. The *Goldfield Chronicle* found a certain irony in the name "Lynchburg" as being the place of birth for "Diamondfield Jack."

68 *Reno Evening Gazette*, March 16, 1908.

69 *Tonopah Daily Bonanza*, March 18, 1908.

WE CAN'T HAVE THE NAVY IN GOLDFIELD BUT DIAMONDFIELD JACK HAS HIS ARSENAL

"DIAMONDFIELD JACK" Davis was born in Lynchburg, Virginia. Odd name that. Anyway, for 37 years Jack has been playing with a gun. At six months he began teething on the dull and deadly barrel of a six-shooter, and every time he gets mad now he whips out one of the four he carries and chews off a hunk of steel that soothes and satisfies him.

Some people in the Wild West think Jack Davis is a "bad" man. He isn't! He's kind, gentle and generous and has a habit of behaving like sticky fly paper in warm weather when a friend is involved. In a pinch, I wouldn't be the least bit afraid of Jack, if I had a drop on him.

Jack has been in every mix-up, personal and political, since the gray-streaked desert began putting on dignified city airs. I am told that it is not prudent to call him "shorter and uglier" nor "particularly mendacious." Remember he's a Virginian, and it's always best to smile when addressing him in the strenuous manner of the West.

A friend of Jack's asked him the other day why he carried four guns, and he replied; "Well, if I ever got into a mix-up and didn't have my guns and got killed I'd never forgive myself as long as I lived."[70]

---

70 *Goldfield Chronicle*, May 2, 1908.

"Diamondfield Jack" Davis Drawing One and with One to Carry.

from the Goldfield Chronicle, May 2, 1908.

Libel! (1909)

In 1909, Davis was back in court—on the plaintiff's side.

"Diamondfield Jack" Davis, a well- known mine operator of Goldfield, will bring a suit for criminal libel against the Curtis Publishing Company for the publication in The Saturday Evening Post of a story which he claims reflects on him. The story is entitled, "The Embarrassing Conduct of Benjamin Ellis, Millionaire," and the author is James Hopper, who spent several weeks here in the boom days. The story attracted much unfavorable comment among Goldfield people at the time of publication.

Hopper chose for his villain one "Diamondfield Jack" and Davis claims that he is widely known by and frequently receives mail addressed to that name. He has forwarded a copy of the offensive publication to district attorney Sam Platt at Carson City, and declares that if he cannot reach and punish the publishing company by a criminal action, he will bring a civil suit.[71]

The only follow-up to the libel suit in the newspapers was a short article published In the *Goldfield Daily Tribune* on January 14, 1909:

"AUTHOR OFFERS APOLOGY TO DIAMONDFIELD JACK"

"In a letter to Frank Tack, the author, James Hopper, says he had no intention of slandering or libeling Jack Davis when he referred in his story to "Diamondfield Jack." The author says he did not have the Goldfield man in mind at all when penning the yarn, and hopes he will believe him."

No other reference was made to the incident so it appears Jack must have accepted the explanation as written.

---

71 *Goldfield Review*, November 14, 1908.

The year 1908 seems to have been Davis' high water mark, and that of Goldfield as well.

The newspapers continued to have many positive reports but new strikes were being reported in surrounding areas in Central Nevada. In the Goldfield district, news focused on the established mines with deep bodies of ore having to be mined by an ever-increasing number of men and more and more expensive and improved equipment. The earlier shallow surface and easy-to-extract ore bodies were being worked out and were closing down. These smaller operators had to either go to work for the larger mine owners or move to the outer areas which were showing promise of the new strikes. The newspapers reported on these new mines or claims being developed. One new gold district named the Pioneer District was reported to be booming and listed Jack Davis as having developed several claims with good shipping grade ore exposed.

Davis explains the fast growth of the new district from his first visit in early December, 1908, when there were but few signs of life and not a single building—but by the end of January there were seven saloons, two stores with two more about to open, and five restaurants. A new discovery near Clifford was reported in the *Goldfield Review*. "Tonopah is excited over a new strike which is reported from the neighborhood of the Belliehelen district, five miles southeast of Clifford."[72]

Jack started to be heard from these new districts more and more starting in mid-1908. Along with the other men from the Goldfield District, Jack moved from different areas announcing good discoveries, at least surface strikes which looked promising.

Davis' misfortunes started in earnest early in January 1909 when Minnie Davis, Jack's wife for nearly five years, sued for divorce. For several months following the announcement Jack was reported to be involved in new developments in the new Pioneer District near Bullfrog and the new claims near Clifford.

Also in January, soon after being sued for divorce, Davis was arrested and charged with jumping property (similar to claim jumping). The property was known as the Hicks Hot Springs and had been purchased jointly by Davis and a man by the name of J.J. Reagan. Reagan claimed that since the purchase the two of them had failed to

72 *Goldfield Review*, February 13, 1909.

pay for the assessment work on the property and lost their claim. Reagan claims he had come back later and homesteaded the land for agricultural purposes and now claimed total ownership. The evidence seems to prove Reagan's claim and the criminal charges against Davis were dropped.

Shortly after these events, Jack left the Goldfield area, and the written record surrounding him turns relatively sparse. Information about his whereabouts and mining activities is picked from newspapers from around the country.

The first indication that he had ventured out from his business interests in the Goldfield region is found in the *Los Angeles Herald* dated May 4, 1910.

"Diamondfield Jack's return from Mexico and the Alamos district of Sonora."

"He was a guest at the Hollenbeck, where he would remain for ten days. Mr. Davis is operating two large properties, one a gold mine and the other a copper mine, located a short distance east of Nova Joa, which is on the Mexican extension of the Southern Pacific."

Some twenty days later the *Tonopah Bonanza* reprinted a three-column article from the *Los Angeles Times* telling about Diamondfield Jack's adventures in Mexico. The writer of the article compares him to a dime novel hero, having been a famous "gun man," a cow puncher, a revolutionist, a miner, a millionaire, and has just returned from an Indian fight with the Yaquis.

When "Diamondfield" happens to be in the hotel lobby relating his adventures you can't tear a bellboy away from the bench with a Chinese war gong. He is a real border character compared to whose feats the greatest movie picture hero is only a spoiled firm."

At the time of the I.W.W. riots at Goldfield, Jack made himself nationally famous by his cool, vivid courage.

On one never-to-be-forgotten afternoon, when Goldfield was surging with a murderous mob and the townspeople were cowering in barricaded rooms, Diamondfield made himself felt.

In the course of the riot someone in the mob happened to break one of Diamondfield's office windows. He came out with a roar like a bull, a six shooter in each hand.

There were in the mob, 500 to 600 armed men; but they turned and fled down the street, stumbling and falling over each other in their haste to get away. Jack chased them for two blocks. Then he stood in the middle of the street flourishing his two revolvers and daring the whole mob to come back and fight. But with each invitation to fight Jack had to raise his voice louder, for his audience was rapidly disappearing never to turn to accept his invite.[73]

Another indication came in a Nevada newspaper: the *State News*, sometime in June 1912, (the date is so smudged it cannot be read) reported the return of C.B. Higginson to Goldfield for a visit.

Higginson, one of the pioneers of the Goldfield District, and considered to be one of the most successful mining men in Southern Nevada, after having visited a large number of mining camps over a wide area of the county, still feels that Goldfield is the best of them all in every way. During his travels he visited the new camp in New Mexico where Diamondfield Jack is now operating and says Jack is now "in the money." The property is located about 15 miles north of Lordsburg. Several old time Goldfield men employed by Davis including Jack Conkling and Al McCormack. They are shipping ore to a smelter and are employing about 40 men on his property.[74]

73 *Tonopah Daily* , reprint from the *Los Angeles Times*, May 21, 1910.

74 *State News, some time in June 1912.*

Wandering the west (1912)

Reports of Davis in those years were varied and not always reliable.

The *El Paso Herald* also reported the mine activity on Steins Pass north of Lordsburg, New Mexico: "Jack "Diamondfield" has quite a force of miners at work and are taking out the richest ore ever struck on the El Oro since it was opened up."[75]

The big news in 1913 was about the "Death of Diamondfield Jack" and then his reappearance a short time later in New York City. The first reports of Jack's death appeared in the *Salt Lake Tribune* March 14, 1913, and spread across the country. The *Tribune* head line: "Diamondfield Jack' Killed, Is Executed in Mexico" Fearless Miner Laughed at Death Warning in Days of Goldfield Trouble."

The *Tribune* reported that according to their sources the killing of Diamondfield Jack had recently occurred in Mexico. Their information indicated "Davis died with his boots on, backed against a wall and shot by a Mexican Federal firing squad."

And on March 15, 1913 a Salt Lake City newspaper reported:

"JACK DAVIS SHOT BY FIRING SQUAD OF FEDERALS"

Notorious Cowboy, Miner, Gunfighter and Soldier of fortune faces firing squad. Adventurer well known here meets Death in Mexican War

DESPERADO IN A SOFTER LIGHT BY DEFENDERS

"Diamondfield Jack" Davis not so bad, they say, as he's been painted.

Soften by the years, declares the Statesman, bullets from the guns of his executioners put an end to the life of "Diamondfield" Jack but no human agency could erase from the record this stirring chapter in Idaho and Nevada history that was written during his celebrated fight for freedom. John Hailey, now the State historian and then warden of the state penitentiary had a different opinion of Jack. He was a

75 *El Paso Herald*, July 3, 1912.

habitual liar and braggart, but to offset those faults he was possessed of an exceedingly tender heart, was liberal and kindly, and his conduct during this time I was at the penitentiary was exemplary in every way. We never had a better-behaved prisoner.

Four days after the *Tribune* report, Jack was reported to be well and safe in New York. A telegram sent to Van De Spaulding, a friend in Salt Lake City, indicated that he was well and requested his friend to wire him $300: "Van, I want you to wire me $300. Wire McAlpin Hotel, New York. Have copper gold mine named August Lordsburg, New Mexico, producing. Am here making deal. Also have half interest in 6000 angora goats. Cannot raise cash on them."

Davis evidently had a sense of humor about the goats.

The *Salt Lake Telegram* reported a few months later that Jack, previously believed dead, was back in Zion greeting friends: "He was in the city and checked into the Semloh Hotel, alive and well. While in the city Jack called on Judge O.W. Powers whom he claims as one of his best friends. Jack explained his good fortune of missing his execution thusly: My execution had been ordered but never accomplished due to the friendship of a peon, who informed me in time to effect an escape."[76]

While Davis was in Salt Lake the *Salt Lake Tribune* reported on July 16, 1913; "Yesterday afternoon Davis called on Judge O.W. Powers and the two men spend a pleasant hour together. Mr. Davis said, last night, that he would in all probability make his future headquarters in Salt Lake.

The most exciting event in Jack's life, other than the seven times he sat in Albion's jail and worried about being hanged, took place in Butte, Montana on Wednesday, September 24, 1913.

This incident was reported by the *Butte Miner* and was then carried by the *Anaconda Standard, Montana Standard, Tonopah Daily Sun, Nevada State Journal* and the *Idaho Statesman*. The *Idaho Statesman* carried a couple follow-up articles as well.

---

76 *Salt Lake Tribune*, July 12, 1913.

Davis owned some mining property in Montana and he was in Butte on business. The trouble Jack encountered in Butte can be traced back to his days in Goldfield, and his conflict with the I. W. W. union, which had held a grudge against Davis since he played a major role in breaking the union's boycott of the town of Goldfield. To compound the union's dislike, Jack was one of the chief witnesses in the conviction of the two union representatives for the murder of the restaurant owner, John Silva. The boycott was back in 1906 and the shooting of Silva happened in March of 1907.

While Davis was in Dave Morgan's saloon in Butte he was approached by a tall man who gave notice that his presence was not wanted in Butte and that he had better get out of town. Davis said he took the warning as coming from the I.W.W., and responded by saying to the man, "I am not yet finished with my business and as soon as I am finished I will be leaving Butte."

One of the news accounts detailed, from Davis' point of view, what happened next.

Davis said, I had gone into this store to see if I could secure a job for a young friend of mine whom I knew in Goldfield. While I was standing talking to the proprietor three men entered. Two were middle aged, one of the two wearing a long coat and cap. The one in the middle was only a youth.

They came up to where I was talking to the clerk and asked for some .25 ammunition. As soon as the clerk turned to get it the man in the middle turned on me and said:

"Now you -----, we have got you!" whipping out his gun while he spoke. I grabbed his arm and jerked my knife out of my pocket. We scuffled for a minute and I caught him a slash in the small of his back behind his kidneys.

I thought my time had come. I kept hold of his coat sleeve, and from the floor I saw the flash of the red streaked buttons of the I. W. W. I kept squirming and lunging at all three of the men, the other two having run up as I struck the floor. I kicked with all my might. After the shot I think I got one of the men a good cut with my knife. I spit out a tooth which the bullet hit. Then I broke loose and ran out the back way.

Davis' entrance into the Finlin Hotel created a sensation. His face was smeared with blood and was dripping from the hole in his jaw. Well, they got me after all, he shouted. Get me a gun and I'll see about this proposition.

Davis' appearance, however, suggested he was in greater need of surgical attention than of artillery, and he was quickly driven to the emergency hospital.[77]

The *Idaho Statesman* printed on the following day a dispatch from the Butte paper.

But Bud Ryan, who "Diamondfield Jack" Davis stabbed Wednesday afternoon when Ryan and two others attempted to deport him, will probably die. To the officers Ryan has made a dying statement, which the authorities will not divulge. Ryan and his companions, all I. W. W.'s, attempted to take Davis out of town by the auto route, a common practice in this camp with strike breakers and non-unionist. They snagged with strong arm work in running up against Davis.

Davis' one regret Thursday was that he did not have a gun with him at the time.

"If I had my six shoot those three fellows would have been occupying slabs in an undertaking shop," he said.

Davis is resting easy despite that a tooth was shot out and his jaw punctured by a bullet with a portion of his tongue clipped out.[78]

Jack's remarks in the above article about, (his only regret was not having my gun) brings to mind his quote in the *Goldfield Chronicle* May 2, 1908. When he was asked by a friend why he carried four guns, and he said, "Well, if I ever got into a mix-up and didn't have my guns and got killed, I'd never forgive myself as long as I lived." There is nothing like a little mishap to make a trip memorable.

---

77 Reported in the *Butte Miner, Anaconda Standard*, and the *Idaho Statesman*, September 25, 1913.

78 *Idaho Statesman*, September 26,1913.

The Industrial Workers of the World were not inclined to let the Butte matter die but instead continued to cause trouble, including threats on Jack's life.

A number of rowdy and boisterous men drifted into Butte a week or so after the shooting incident, continuing their threats and in general causing trouble. They were reported to be working their way southbound to Salt Lake "to get Diamondfield Jack Davis."

An article in the *Idaho Statesman* on October 18, 1913 reported:

INDUSTRAL WORKERS AFTER DIAMONDFIELD JACK DAVIS AGAIN

Butte, Mont. The band of 16 Industrial Workers of the World were arrested in this city Friday and released amid shouts of Socialists who filled the courtroom. The men later seized an Oregon Short Line box car, defying the train crew, and riding as far as Dillon, where they were clubbed out of that town after a battle with officers. They are en route to Salt Lake for the purpose of "getting" Diamondfield Jack Davis according to information which leaked out in Industrial Workers circles here Friday. The workers here stated they were going to Salt Lake to free a prisoner, but no significance was attached to the remark.

That was their slogan, the meaning of which, it is said "to get Davis." The band is working its way out of southern Montana southbound for Salt Lake. The workers a short time ago were released from the Minot, North Dakota jail.[79]

On October 29 a similar incident happened in Sparks, Nevada, where nineteen I.W. W. men were forcibly removed by the police from a box car which these men had commandeered, perhaps as far east as Salt Lake—although Davis wasn't even there. "There was some indication the load of men were connected in some way to Jack Davis and the trouble reported in Butte 10 days earlier."[80]

As Davis aged and his fortunes diminished, he continued to make periodic appearances across the county. In 1914 he was reported to be in the Las Vegas area inspecting mining properties, and a couple of

79 *Idaho Statesman*, October 18, 1913.

80 *Reno Evening Gazette*, October 29, 1913.

weeks later he was in Death Valley involved in the Carbonite Mine which was high in gold, silver, and copper.

The *Idaho Statesman* did not give up on their position that Jack was guilty, nor did they hide their political bias towards Hawley and the Democrats. During the 1914 political campaign in the Boise area Hawley was involved in the governor's race, and the *Statesman* (Oct 29, 1914) railed against Mr. Hawley. "Mr. Hawley cannot escape from his "cash value" foolishness with which Mr. Hawley inflicted on the people of Idaho at tremendous cost to them. The people cannot forget the Democratic record on prison scandal and the "Diamondfield Jack" Davis and Corcoran pardons."

The *Statesman* refused to concede what the evidence proved, evidence that changed the minds of Cassia County's Prosecuting Attorney and convinced Special Prosecuting Attorney Judge Orlando W. Powers that Jack was in fact innocent. It continued to back William Borah's position of maintaining Jack's guilt.

A handwritten note can be found in the Idaho Historical Society's archives, with Borah's signature and addressed to 'Cal'—almost certainly Calvin Cobb, the owner and publisher of the *Idaho Statesman* at the time and a longtime friend of Senator Borah. The postmark date on the note was Nov 16th with no year indicated. It may not have been intended to refer specifically to the Jack Davis issue but does reflect a characteristic and attitude which Borah maintained through his whole career, that once he took a position or made up his mind he rarely changed positions or his mind. The handwritten note reads:

"My Dear Cal,

Do you like Crow? If you do you can eat it. I do not like it and I am not going to eat it. I am through.

[signed] Borah"

On November 23, 1913, just two months after Jack's brush with death in Butte, Montana, his picture appeared on the front page of the *Salt Lake Tribune*. Davis along with a Salt Lake County Deputy and a Salt Lake City Patrolman participated in a manhunt for the man suspected of killing the chief of police from Bingham and a county deputy while they were attempting to arrest the man suspected of having killed another man.

The article describes Jack Davis and Patrolman Lester Wire as expert marksmen. The two marksmen were being transported by automobile to the area where the fugitive was being chased down by foot and horseback. The fugitive was on foot and out maneuvered the posse for five days and over fifty miles round trip only to end up back in Bingham where the chase began. The fugitive's name was Rafael Lopez and he disappeared in to a mine shaft in Bingham Canyon reported to have 10 miles of honeycomb tunnels and eleven entrances. Attempts were made to search the mine for Lopez and even smoke him out with no success. Lopez somehow escaped and was not heard of again. The case remained open for ninety years until January 24, 2003 when Deputy Sheriff Randy Lish requested to pick up the search again. His research led him to the biography of the legendary Texas Ranger Frank Hamer. There it was learned Frank Hamer was part of a group of lawmen sent down near the Mexican border to kill or capture Rafael Lopez. Lopez's luck ran out in late 1921. The Texas Rangers knew of Lopez's Utah history but the information was never relayed to the Utah authorities. This finally closed the file on the largest and longest manhunt in Utah's history.

In 1915 Davis was reported to be operating in the Amalie mining district near Bakersfield, California. Later in the year he was reported to be in El Paso, Texas along with investors from Chicago and Los Angeles buying five claims with promising results.

During these years Davis seemed to get by financially, continually working on new mining ventures. The trick was to find a property or a claim that looked promising and then find investors with the eternal hope the next venture would be the one to strike it rich. It happened often enough over the years that money always seemed to be available to try one more time.

On March 9, 1916 the *Idaho Statesman* reported, "Jack Davis is now operating in California Fields—Davis has the "Tom Reed apex" and other properties in the Oatman district, and also a large copper property south of Needles, in the Whippe range, which he will start developing at once, and will be joined by Charles Sparks, son of the late Governor Sparks of Nevada."

On January 5, 1918, the *Goldfield News & Weekly Tribune* announced:

"DIAMONDFIELD JACK" HAS FOUND A WINNER, GOLDFIELD PIONEER IS WORKING GOOD VEIN NEAR CARSON.

Jack Davis and his associates are developing half a dozen mining claims beyond Carson Lake being seven or eight miles south of Allen Springs. It is an entirely new discovery. The news spread to several other papers about the rich veins he was working on in the Carson Lake district.

Jack must have remained in the Fallen, Hazen, and Carson Lake area for the rest of the year, according to an interview which the Reno Evening Gazette conducted with Jack on December 31, 1918.

"Diamondfield Jack" Davis dropped into Reno from his present headquarters at Hazen yesterday with some good-looking specimens of Quartz and some oil sand in his pocket, but he did not care to discuss his own mining. He was willing to talk about the weather, the effect of the dry law or almost anything else, but not a word would he say about his claims and prospects.

We buried John Barleycorn decently and well at Hazen, said Davis, and he is very dead there. I do not agree with my dry friends on the subject, but submit to the will of the majority as every good American always does—that is, we bury the hatchet but leave the handle sticking out so we can grasp it again if the law ever gives us a chance."

"No miner, however he may feel about the use and abuse of liquor, has anything against the saloon man. I have had thirty-six years' experience with them and know that in every mining camp they grubstake and they dug and they put up the where-withal to start new propositions."[81]

Back on February 26, 1918 the *Goldfield News & Weekly Tribune* did run an article about oil shale being found in Nevada, and Davis's involvement with that: "FIND OIL SHALE NEAR EASTGATE. "DIAMONDFIELD JACK" DAVIS ON GROUND AT NEW DISCOVERY"

81 *Reno Evening Gazette*, December 31, 1918.

However, the article said Jack had only visited the site of the discovery and reported it to the paper.

In 1927 the *Idaho Statesman* ran a story about Diamondfield from Fresno, California. The story was picked up by the Associated Press and carried a photo of Jack. No matter where he was, his reputation and something about his past followed him. The story, in part, went as follows:

"Diamondfield Jack" Davis who lives on his Spring Mountain mining claim in Nevada, is not a superstitious man. A front seat at gold stampedes and opera bouffe, revolution in Central America has taken away his faith in rabbits' feet and his awe of black cats.

But this survivor of gun-fighting days of the west does believe in seven as his lucky number.

Seven times Diamondfield Jack, who got his name in the hard stone regions of South Africa, has heard an Idaho judge set the time and place of his hanging. Seven times he was taken back to his cell and there listened to the ring of hammers on his gallows, while outside the barred door the death watch stood guard.

Then after seven years of jail life while his attorneys fought to save him, he stepped into the sunshine a free man, by the act of Governor Hunt.

Now near the end of the long trail, Diamondfield Jack has no regrets, he says, over fortunes which might have been his or glory lost. His one lament is over wearing of false teeth. Those nature gave him were shot out in a labor war in Butte, Montana., in 1914—merely an incident in a perilous career."[82]

Davis was often ready to boast or at least talk as a big promoter of the next big boom. The *Tonopah Daily Times-Bonanza* carried an article typical of a Jack Davis promotion from a Carson City paper dated December 3, 1929.

Jack Davis, "Diamondfield Jack", one of the pioneer boomers of Tonopah and Goldfield, bad man, good man, prospector, and man of

82 *Idaho Statesman*, December 11, 1927.

fortune and misfortune, is spending a couple of days here, says the Carson Appeal where he was called to look over some mining property of a friend.

Jack, as many paint him, is generally loaded down with artillery. On the contrary he laid aside the side arms and comes in with ordinary clothes, well kept, somewhat fatter than during the fighting days of the rush, and is just looking after mines and mining.

At present his address is Las Vegas which he declares is to become the city of the west and will probably take in part of Los Angeles.

He confesses to pushing up against the 70 mark in age but declines to grow old, claiming that he is just reaching his prime and is quieting down enough to look after business and stop fussing around on booms.

"When I come back in a few weeks, I'll tell you the layout, it's the biggest thing uncorked since the Mohawk and will last twice as long," was his remark as he met Governor Balzar and left the reporter.

Reunions and Endings (1938)

According to the *Sacramento Times* dated July 10, 1938, Jack paid a visit to Frank Jordan, then Secretary of State for the State of California.

'Diamondfield' Jack Davis, who has mined in the Sierras, conspired in Mexico and struck it rich in Brazil, is at 75 still trying to coax hidden wealth from the ground.

The colorful mining character let it be known he hasn't given up when he visited his old friend, Secretary of State Frank C. Jordan, at the capital the other day.

"Diamondfield," said the 78 year-old official, himself a mining man, "I thought you died four years ago. Last I heard of you, you were dead around Tonopah."

"I've been dead a good many times," replied Davis with a chuckle. "But I promised myself long ago I'd outlive you. I just dropped around to see if you were still keeping me alive."

"Diamondfield" had come into town with a sack of ore which he wanted analyzed for tungsten. He said he continues to have crews of prospectors in the hills—back of Bakersfield, between here and Reno, and some in Nevada."

"He's made more fortunes than I can recall," Jordan said after Davis had left.

The Secretary of State's first encounter with Davis was in Goldfield, he recalled. A mob was trying to lynch a murderer and the Sheriff had cold feet.

Well, he said, "Diamondfield" walked out in front of the jail, drew a line in the dust with the barrel of the gun and announced:

There'll be law in Goldfield tonight. The first man who crosses the line dies.

The state executive, remembering Davis' parting boast that he was going to make another fortune in beryllium.[83]

83 *Los Angeles Times*, July 10, 1938.

There was very little news about Jack for several years after his visit with Jordan.

But there was a reunion with one of the most colorful people to cross his path.

Sometime during 1944, Davis learned one of his old girl friends, Evelyn Hildegard, was residing in Boise, Idaho. Hildegard was affectionately known as "Diamond Tooth Lil" in the Idaho city and the Boise area. Jack made contact with Lil and arranged a reunion with her in Las Vegas. The reunion, held in early 1945 made the newspaper around the western United States with headlines similar to this:

Notorious Diamondfield Jack, Boise Sweetheart Hold Reunion in Las Vegas

By 1945 Las Vegas was developing into a city of entertainment and legalized gambling as well as a major center for shipping supplies to mining districts in southern Nevada and the eastern regions of southern California.

In 1906 during the height of the glory days of Goldfield, Nevada, Evelyn Hildegard was attracted to the night life of Goldfield. Saloons and dance halls, with men being paid good wages, were attractive to the talented beautiful lady. She was born with the attributes for success. She was smart and possessed the ability to invest her money in enterprises where she used her singing and dancing talents.

While in Goldfield she met a soon-to-be lifelong friend, Jack Davis, who she described as a fancy dresser who liked to gamble and always wore diamonds and two guns. "Those were in the days when money was free," she said. It was during that period of her life she acquired the nickname "Diamond Tooth Lil," a name she wore with much pride. When asked, she would explain that on a trip to Reno she won a bet with a dentist, for which the payoff was a tooth capped with gold, with a diamond set in the gold.

Lil had come to Goldfield from the Barbary Coast in San Francisco. The San Francisco earthquake and fire prompted her move to Goldfield. Arriving in Goldfield, she bought a dance hall across the street from a café owned by Davis. Lil admitted to having married nine different men but admitted to only one divorce. Davis is said to have been one of the nine.

"Diamond Tooth" Lil, 1945. (photo courtesy Idaho Historical Society)

From Goldfield "Diamond Tooth Lil" first moved to Greenwater, near Death Valley, California, only to discover that the town was dying. So she moved on to Reno, Nevada, where she had a three-year champagne bust and a diamond set in her tooth.

Sometime after 1910, after her three years in Reno, Lil moved to Idaho and landed in Silver City, only to discover that Silver City's heyday was in the 1880s and 1890s. The decline of Silver City was more gradual in nature, though, and that mining town survived up until World War II. Lil eventually moved into Boise and pretty much ended her days as a madam. She first owned the Boise Star Rooming House and later the Depot Inn.[84]

With the passage of time, one's priorities change, and recalling old memories sometimes takes precedence over making new ones. It was this time in both Jack's and Lil's lives when rekindling of these memories became important to them. Jack and Lil both admitted that each wondered about the other's whereabouts.

Sometime in 1944 the *Idaho Statesman* featured an interview with Lil about her life; it may have been picked up by other regional papers as well. At that point, Jack had been living in seclusion in Las Vegas and Los Angeles for some years, but he became aware of the article and learned of Lil's current place of residence, so he made contact with her in Boise. It had been 30 years since they had been together. Lil, in fact, thought Jack was dead, so she was glad to hear from him again and decided to visit him.

Lil made the trip to Las Vegas during the latter part of December 1944. She planned to go to Los Angeles to spend the winter with friends, so the trip to Las Vegas was on her way to California. Jack and Lil met in an appropriate setting, in a gambling hall thick with smoke, with men lined up at the bar. Davis was characteristically at a poker table with silver dollars stacked in front of him when the lady from Boise stepped over to the table and greeted him.

Thirty years had changed the features of both, but as the *Idaho Statesman* reported on the reunion on January 19, 1945, Diamondfield said, "There's only one woman in all this land with a diamond in her front tooth and she's my dream girl."

"Remember when" was the way their conversation started out, and then another "remember when"—and so it went. "We have much to talk over all right," the two agreed at their reunion.[85]

---

84 Information about Lil's life taken from *The Life and Times of Death Valley's Diamondtooth Lil*, by Robin Flinchum.

85 Quotes taken from *Salt lake Tribune* dated January 19, 1945.

Jack Davis, 1938. (photo from newspaper)

This reunion symbolized the dying embers of the historic era of the taming of the West.

Harnessing the West required a robust, strong-willed class of men and women able to handle trials, isolation, loneliness, and the inconvenience of living without the amenities and comforts already enjoyed in the East. This era witnessed a mass migration of people moving across the vast continent—a conglomeration of adventurous souls, religious freedom seekers, escaping law breakers, fortune seekers, broken spirits, those displaced after the Civil War, and thousands of others going West just because they were poor and wanted free land. In most cases law enforcement, the judicial system, and civility were slow to follow the mass migration of all these human beings, each protecting his own newly- acquired territory. How all these different factions learned to live together makes for the rich and fascinating history of which the West is most proud.

"Diamondfield Jack" and "Diamond-tooth Lil" represent just a few of the many episodes which contribute to the fascination of the Western lore. Jack and Lil did not just live during the era; in a very real sense they helped create what we now refer to as the "Wild Wild West." Their vivid legacy allows us to experience a little of the feelings of the people and to relive, to a small extent, the history of that fascinating period.

Death by taxi (1949)

You could expect the life of Jack Davis, "Diamondfield Jack," to end as a result of some extraordinary circumstance or event that at least matched his exceptional history.

Davis, in fact, must have had more than nine lives. Operating on both sides of the law, he had been pursued by the law as a suspected murderer and twice pursued suspected murderers while on the side of the law. He faced a deadline to be hanged seven different times for a murder he was accused of committing. He had faced an angry mob with weapons drawn defending an accused murderer He defended three paper boys from an angry mob. He was ordered to face a firing squad but escaped. He bore the scar of a bullet on his left calf just below the knee. He survived an assassin's bullet to his jaw, and went through life cloaked with a reputation of being the bad guy. He experienced wealth, fame, business partnerships with bankers, two governors,and three U.S. Senator,s and a broken fortune.

On December 28, 1949, while walking on a sidewalk in Las Vegas, Davis stepped down off the curb and was struck by a taxi cab which was backing up.

During his trip to the hospital, he told his friend riding with him that he was going to get well and would live to be 100 years old. He exonerated the taxi cab driver, telling the police how he had stepped off the curb and into the path of the cab without looking. Jack lay in the hospital until Sunday morning, January 2, 1949, when he passed away quietly.

It was several days before the news reached Idaho via the *Deseret News* out of Salt Lake City (January 6, 1949).

Las Vegas: Funeral services were conducted for Jackson Lee "Diamondfield" Davis 85, last of the west's bad men, Wednesday at 11 a.m. at the Bunkers' Brothers chapel.

The colorful figure of Nevada's mining boom died Sunday at Clark County hospital after being struck by a taxicab.

Davis is said to have made several fortunes and lost them in addition to over a million dollars left to him by his father. He was born in New Jersey 85 years ago and moved to Texas as a young man.

His career involved such things as walking out of the Idaho State prison with a parole seconds before he was scheduled to be executed for murder. He claimed to have been a leading figure in at least one Mexican revolution.

An institution in the early days of Goldfield, Nevada, he was closely identified with such mining camps as Rawhide, Bullfrog, Rhyolite, Tonopah and other camps that made Nevada's past so colorful.

Davis has no known survivors. He was buried by old friends at the Woodlawn Cemetery. The Rev. Thomas Daley, of the United Lutheran Church, officiated during the service.

The irony of this obituary is that a number of facts about Davis' life are misstated.

Perhaps this is fitting, though, as a way to send to his grave evidence of Jack going through life not always telling the truth himself. His age is listed in the death notice as 85, but according to the prison records of February 27, 1899, the day he was booked into the penitentiary, he listed his age as 28 years, seven months. The prison record would establish his birth date as July 1870, which would have made him 79 years old at the time of his death in 1949. He listed his birth place as West Virginia on the prison record in 1899; the obituary listed his birth place as New Jersey. The obituary reported that Jack walked out of prison with a parole seconds before he was scheduled to be executed for murder. The fact was, he was in the penitentiary at the time serving a life term as a result of having his death sentence commuted to life in prison 17 months earlier.

Searching for the truth about the life of Jack Davis has been my motivation for this whole story.

At the last, part of the truth which Davis knew but never completely revealed was buried in the grave at the Woodlawn Cemetery in Las Vegas. Where was he born and what year was he born? Was he ever married and did he have a son?

There will remain in the minds of many the guilt of Jack Davis and in many the belief that he was a victim of an injustice caused in part by his own doing and in part by the actions and over reactions of the sheepmen and cattlemen. Too often emotions override civility, resulting in confused reasoning which leads to increased conflict and contention between the parties, often leading to injuries or even death. In Jack Davis's case, there is plenty of blame to be shared by all parties.

Over the years the "Diamondfield" Jack story has grown from an unfortunate incident in the history of Cassia County and the state of Idaho into a legend, with a sometimes mythical and even a romantic image. Jack Davis was, in fact, an intriguing individual who created a legacy that will live on in Western folklore for years to come.

Jack Davis' headstone. (photo by author)

A legal time line

Time line of the legal procedures which James Hawley initiated on behalf of Jack Davis during his fight for freedom after his arrest, March 1897 until his pardon, December 18, 1902.

February 4, 1896	**John Wilson & Daniel Cummins Killed**	**February 1899**	**Jack Davis was transferred to state penitentiary**
March 2, 1896	Jack Davis & Fred Gleason Charged with Murder	October 19, 1899	9th Circuit Court of Appeals refused a Habeas Corpus
March 1897	Davis & Gleason Arrested in Yuma, AZ & MT	December 1899	Idaho Supreme Court ruled that Davis's execution had to be in Albion under old law
April 5, 1897	Davis & Gleason Arraigned for Murder	December 1899	Davis transferred back to Cassia County jail
April 8, 1897	The Davis Trial Begins in court house at Albion	March 26, 1900	9th Circuit Court petitioned for a Writ of Habeas Corpus directed to Cassia County Sheriff
April 15, 1897	Jury returns guilty verdict Death Penalty	April 2, 1900	9th Circuit refused petition but appeal forwarded to U.S. Supreme Court
April 24, 1897	Judge Stockslager-sentenced Davis to die on June 4, 1897	April 2, 1900	9th Circuit Court stayed all proceedings
April 1897	Gleason was tried & acquitted	December 23, 1900	U.S. Supreme Court affirmed Lower Courts decision
May 3, 1897	Motion for a new trial, sentence suspended until hearing	April 1901	Hawley moved for a new trial in Cassia County.
January 12,	Judge Stockslager	April 1901	District Judge

1898	refuses Davis a new trial		Steward denied the motion for a new trial.
January 18,1898	Hawley files with Idaho Supreme Court for new trial	April 1901	Davis was resentenced to hang on June 21, by Steward
March 1898	Hawley files briefs with Idaho Supreme Court	April 25,1901	Appealed to ID. Supreme Ct. certificate of probable cause.
June 16,1898	Idaho Supreme Court sustains lower Court decision	June 17,1901	Idaho Supreme Court refused to intervene
July 25,1898	Application to the Idaho Board of Pardons for pardon	June 17,1901	Board of Pardons changed hanging date to July 3,1901
September 1898	Idaho Supreme Court resentence Davis to hang on October 21, 1898	July 1,1901	Board of Pardons met all day on the 1st and the 2^{nt} without a decision as to pardon
September 22,1898	Governor Steunenberg granted Davis a reprieve until December 16, 1898.	July 3,1901	The board moved the date of hanging to July 17th.
October 13,1898	James E. Bower confesses to his part in the killing of Wilson and Cummins	July 16, 1901	The Board Of Pardons commuted Davis's sentence to life imprisonment.
December 1898	The Board of Pardons granted Davis a reprieve until February 1,1899	December 4, 1901	The Idaho Supreme Court refused to overturn the conviction of Jack Davis.
January 22, 1899	Board of Pardons refuses the pardon for Jack Davis.	December 5, 1901 thru December 17, 1902	Davis was imprisoned at State Penitentiary.
January 23, 1899 January 28, 1899	Board resentences Jack to hang February 1, 1999 Applied to Circuit Court of Appeal for a habeas corpus.	December 18, 1902	The pardon came late on the 17th left the prison a free man on the 18th.

January 31, 1899	Circuit Court of Appeals issues a stay of execution	Late 1902 early 1903	Jack went to Tonopah, NV in search of a new life.
February 1, 1899	Stay of execution received in Albion the morning of planned execution	For a number of years after 1903	Diamondfield Jack struck it rich with mining claims. He made millions but lost it
1899 Legislature session	A law passed that all executions had to be in Boise.	December 28, 1948 and January 2, 1949	Jack was hit by a taxi in Las Vegas and died on Jan 2nd.
February 17,1899	Jeff Gray' Trial held in Albion		

Acknowledgements

If it takes a village to raise a child, it takes more than a village to write a book. I quickly learned just how much help is required to hopefully produce a product worthy of all the encouragement and efforts of so many friends

The first person I need to thank is my wife Clydene, and of course my family. Without their faith and encouragement I would never have finished this four-year project. I am sure Clydene sat back and thought I was on another of my many tangents and hobby pursuits I enjoy. I had to get used to that occasional look I received when I would say to people, I am writing a book. That look which said, "You're writing a book? Sure you are!"

I gained a whole new appreciation for the folks working in our libraries and history centers. They – and this includes the city libraries and state historical and archival libraries – have been, without exception, happy and willing to assist every way possible. Many thanks to Janet Gillimore, Executive Director at the Idaho State Historical Society, and Rod House, Administrator of the Public Archives and Research Library in Idaho. Thanks to their entire Staff for their assistance, encouragement, and friendship.

As my research moved into Nevada I again experienced the willing helpfulness from individuals at the Nevada State Historical Society; Heidi Englund at the Reno office, the Staff at the Carson City office, and many thanks to Eva LaRue at the Tonopah office. Due to the fact Jack Davis lived in or near Tonopah for a number of years the Central Nevada Museum and Historical Society had the largest collection of information about "Diamondfield Jack." Eva was able to gather together nearly 200 pieces of useful information for me.

During my early search and research trips looking for information I was assisted by some good friends and other individuals wanting to help and willing to give me valuable information. Alex Kunkel, a local rancher and member of the Twin Falls Historical Society, was most helpful during my efforts to locate and identify the site of the shooting. I appreciated Rich Wills accompanying me on the first unsuccessful search for the camp site near Rogerson. I was finally able to find the camp site of the two sheepherders with the assistance of David L.Curtis, P.E. and his GPS, plus some ground work. Dave has continued to help me by reading parts of the manuscript as I progressed in my writing. Dave and I also took a trip to Carson City, Nevada to do research in the Nevada Archives Library. The visit to Tonopah and the Central Nevada Historical Museum and to Las Vegas to view Jack's grave was made even more enjoyable having Bert Stevenson accompany me.

I am deeply grateful for MaryLou Molitor and the many hours she spent reading and editing for me. She has been close to this project from the start. Marylou and I worked together in the Idaho State Legislature so she had to do a lot of listening to me talk about it, perhaps, to the point of nausea.

My daughter-in-law Kyra has helped me read and make suggestions and corrections which have been appreciated and welcomed. She also was very helpful solving what was to me numerous computer problems, but to her it was just a matter of saying, "oh you just pressed the wrong key again and made the screen go blank so you didn't lose your whole two years of work."

Thanks to my son Jeff for his help arranging and rearranging parts of the story on the computer. His time was greatly appreciated.

Others I am indebted to for help and guidance: Jamie and Joseph Larsen have been very helpful and insightful in my search. Jamie is a relative of Daniel Cummins, one of the young sheep herders killed, and shared with me some wonderful insights from her family history. Jamie's husband, Joseph (Joe), the current Cassia County Clerk, was able to retrieve a picture taken and published in the local newspaper at the trial of "Diamondfield" Jack Davis. Joe has been able to restore the faded 115 year picture into a beautiful framed picture of the event. I have included his restored picture on page 52 in the book.

Verlene Powell from Albion has been a great researcher into the history of Albion, including the Diamondfield Jack trial; Betty Warr at the Oakley Museum; John Taffin a noted arms and munitions expert; Sally Jones relative of Jeff Gray, a central figure in the Davis trial; Patrick McBeaken relative to James E. Bower, also central in the trial and ensuing legal battle of "Diamondfield" Jack case; Laird Noh, a local rancher and sheepman.

And Larry Tomlinson for his assistance in adding the photos in the book and other very helpful assistance with the final book arrangements.

About the author

Max C. Black was born and raised in a farming and mining family in Delta, Utah. After graduating from the University of Utah he moved to Idaho where he has lived since. He operated his own business for twenty years in Boise. Upon selling his business to Key Bank in 1991 he decided to run for the Idaho State Legislature, and served in the House of Representatives for 20 years.

Max has always had a strong interest in history, making a number of trips to study the Civil War. Idaho history has also been of special interest since moving to Idaho. The research into the true history of Jack Davis has consumed his spare time for the past five years.

More on Idaho history at Ridenbaugh Press

The Intermediary by Linn Tull Cannell

What happens when cultures clash, and one person tries to get them to live together? Introducing William Craig, who tried to broker peace between native Nez Perces and newcomers from the East. Craig's story takes us from his flight from Virginia to his days as a mountain man to the Nez Perce conflicts. 15 years in the making, written by an Orofino historian, this is one of the most dramatic stories of early Northwest history.

Idaho 100: The People Who Most Influenced the Gem State by Randy Stapilus and Martin Peterson

Idaho 100, about the 100 most influential people ever in Idaho, by Randy Stapilus and Martin Peterson, will be released in early October. Order by September 29 and be one of the first people to receive it – *and* get a free e-book (pdf) of the *Idaho Political Field Guide*. Both only $15.95 plus shipping.

Upstream by Randy Stapilus

The Snake River Basin Adjudication is one of the largest water adjudications the United States has ever seen, and it may be the most successful. Here's how it happened, from the pages of the *SRBA Digest*, for 16 years the independent source.

See more about these books at Ridenbaugh Press online bookstore: http://www.ridenbaugh.com/index.php/ridenbaugh-book-store/

RIDENBAUGH
PRESS

10034577R00126

Made in the USA
San Bernardino, CA
04 April 2014